A ... HAUNTED HOUSE.

Patricia saw the crying boy, and one day Kathleen reported having seen a woman, dressed in old-fashioned clothes, hovering by the coal cellar. Mrs. McGuire has seen a woman peering in the kitchen window too, but the most frequent manifestation the family reports is the crying, and the sounds of restless feet walking upstairs.

The McGuires had a pet dog, but eventually they had to give him to friends.

Why?

"Twice he jumped through windows, for no reason," Mrs. McGuire told one newspaper reporter who got wind of the haunted house in Lowell. "Once he went through a screen door. I've been told dogs hear things we don't."

And the McGuires have already heard as much as they want to hear . . .

DOCUMENTED TALES OF THE
THAT'S INCREDIBLE!
VOL. 1
UNEXPECTED

THAT'S INCREDIBLE! VOL. 1

Based on the television series created by Alan Landsburg

COMPILED AND WRITTEN BY WENDY JEFFRIES

DESIGNED BY TONY GRECO

A JOVE BOOK

Copyright ©1980 by Ahmel Corporation

All rights reserved. No part of this publication
may be reproduced or transmitted in any form or
by any means, electronic or mechanical, including
photocopy, recording, or any information storage
and retrieval system, without permission in
writing from the publisher.

Requests for permission to make copies of any part
of the work should be mailed to: Permissions,
Jove Publications, Inc., 200 Madison Avenue,
New York, NY 10016

First Jove edition published December 1980

10   9   8   7   6   5   4   3   2   1

Printed in the United States of America

Jove books are published by Jove Publications, Inc.,
200 Madison Avenue, New York, NY 10016

CONTENTS

INTRODUCTION BY ALAN LANDSBURG / 7

1. THE COBRA: CONQUERED KING? / 11
2. CAR JUMPER! / 29
3. STRUCK BY LIGHTNING! (eight times lucky) / 37
4. PAINLESS DENTIST / 45
5. BEAT THE CHICKEN! / 57
6. THE FIRE INSIDE / 63
7. LIFE ON MAN / 77
8. THE HAUNTED HOUSE OF LOWELL, MASS. / 85
9. BEES! BEES! BEES! / 99
10. LOST CHILD? / 113
11. INSIDE TINY TEARS / 121
12. DAVID'S DREAM / 131
13. GHOSTLY ADOPTION SERVICE / 149
14. CLOSE ENCOUNTER / 165
15. THE SMART PILL AND THE MOUSE / 183

INTRODUCTION BY ALAN LANDSBURG

Ten years ago ESP was part of the language of science fiction. As a journalist I was laughed at when I proposed to embark on a serious study of extrasensory perception. Was it possible, I wanted to know, for events that were about to take place to be envisioned? Would ESP let us predict the future? Could we witness something that went on thousands of miles away? When I pointed out to news editors that valid experiments were going on in this field, I was given one of those "too bad he's crazy" looks.

I am glad to report that the incredible is with us, that all of the hobgoblins have been taken out of the world of UFO spotting, yoga trances, and remote viewing experiments. These and other unusual events are being subjected to modern scientific investigation. In a world where we have come to accept cloning as an available medical art, just slightly beyond the modern scientific horizon, life extension through cryogenics as a slim possibility, and real communication with other animal species a practical matter, it's time to say we live amid incredible wonders.

I am proud that my popular television show has provided a means to catalog the serious as well as the frivolous stories of unexplainable events. I delight in reporting the medical wonders, the scientific breakthroughs, and the unusual cases where an individual mind has healed a body. I am pleased we can explore the possibility that such things as ghosts may in some form exist, and I feel privileged to have the opportunity to pose the incredible mysteries that bedevil all of us. From the events at Lowell, Mass. to the arrival of a UFO on a Minnesota roadway, the more we explore the incredible, the more incredible things we find. I hope that each story will be as intriguing to you as it has been to me.

THAT'S INCREDIBLE!

THAT'S INCREDIBLE!
VOL. 1

1 THE COBRA: CONQUERED KING?

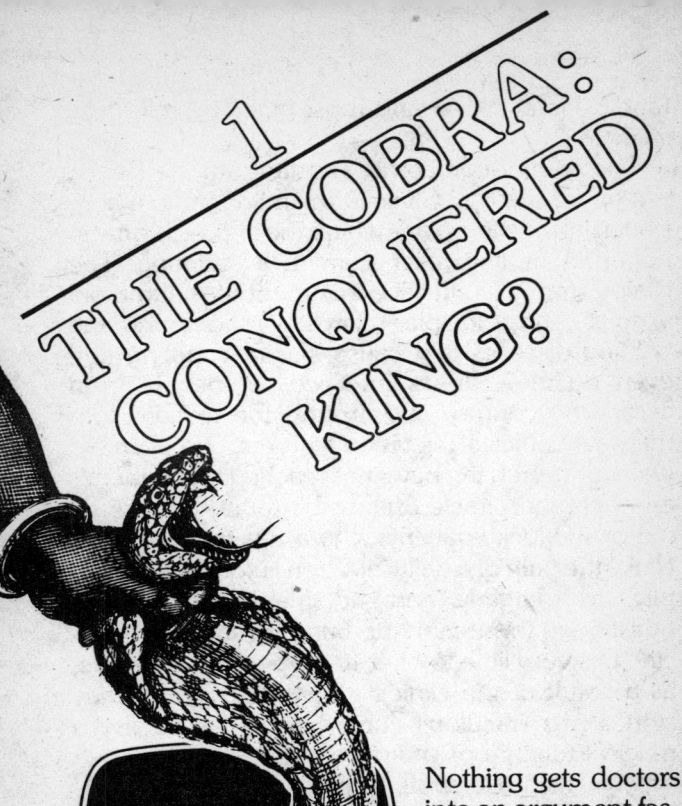

Nothing gets doctors into an argument faster than the notion—or even the news—of a miracle cure. But it could just be that such a wonderful potion actually exists, and as word of it spreads, doctors are starting to argue less... and listen more.

Of course, a miracle cure is incredible under any circumstances, but this one is just a little more amazing than most because it comes from one of man's (and beast's) oldest and most bitter enemies, the snake.

The commotion comes mostly from the Ben J. Sheppard Medical Clinic in Miami, Florida, a controversial meeting-place where the afflicted come in hopes of finding relief from their suffering. The clinic's strangely effective treatment of rheumatoid arthritis and multiple sclerosis—two cruel and baffling diseases that cause severe crippling and even death— draws hundreds of people from across the country and around the world. From magazine articles, television features, and plain old word-of-mouth the news has reached them: there's an apparent miracle drug to be found here.

For the lucky patients who are taken on by the clinic, the pain of a daily injection is something happily, even eagerly, endured. Many doctors have questioned this treatment, but conventional medicine has very little to offer these people. And here, as a result of the clinic's efforts, there are many stories of miraculous cures brought about by a magical mixture of snake venoms.

"I've had 102 shots to date," says one elderly lady, and at a rate of one shot per day that means she's been coming to the clinic 102 days. "Before I had the shots there were shoes I could not get on because my feet were so swollen and my ankles, too. My whole body was swollen. But I have none of that now, no swelling whatsoever, and the pain has been minimized to practically none at all." As she speaks, she receives her hundred-and-third injection of the snake-venom serum.

The treatment does more than simply reduce swelling, *much* more.

"When I first came to the clinic," says a younger

THAT'S INCREDIBLE!

woman, "I walked like this." She hunches her shoulders and walks stiffly, her legs dragging. Children might say she was walking like Frankenstein's Monster trying to imitate Igor. "My arm just hung there, and I would pick it up and put it down, pick it up and put it down. I started on the serum on October 3, 1978, and I can do anything now." She twirls in circles like a ballet dancer, and the change seems almost impossible. "I teach exercise to the other multiple sclerosis patients who come into the clinic, and I can go dancing." Her face is brilliant with joy and triumph. "I can do anything," she says.

Dr. Stanley Van den Noort, Chariman of Research for the Multiple Sclerosis Society of America, gives the typical response to the idea of such a miracle drug: "It is very difficult to evaluate any new treatment for a chronic disease," he says sternly. "The dilemma that we get into is that, if you have a chronic disabling illness, that is associated with a feeling of being down or depressed in relationship to the illness.

"You are very eager to find almost anything that will produce improvement, and when something is advocated for treatment, such as a snake venom, and applied to a chronic disease such as multiple sclerosis, more than half the people who get that treatment—regardless of what it is—will get better. But that dramatic improvement is probably largely psychological in nature."

Perhaps Dr. Van den Noort is right, but it's difficult to believe the progress claimed by the "ballet dancer" is all in her mind. Dr. Van den Noort's comments on the snake-venom treatment arelike many made by medical men, but then they *could* be slightly prejudiced—as history tells us they have always been—against a miracle created by the kind of researcher doctors resent the most: a layman, with no medical training. And it was such a layman who first caught on to the uses of snake venom.

The man's name is Bill Haast, and if you ever need to reach him—which we hope you'll never

THAT'S INCREDIBLE!

need to do—you'll find him at the Miami Serpenterium.

A giant sculpture of a king cobra, his hood majestically expanded, greets visitors at the entrance to the Serpenterium, which Bill Haast founded in

THAT'S INCREDIBLE!

1948. It looks like just another roadside attraction, a tourist grabber, and it's a fact that many visitors to the Serpenterium leave the place without ever knowing the important work that goes on there.

True, there's much for tourists to see: an incredible collection of snakes—almost too many kinds to count, and each more deadly than the last—and many other reptiles as well. And in a special pit, in front of a throng of enthralled spectators, a man in a white suit handles an enormous king cobra with a long hook—which is still too close for comfort, or at least most people would think so. This brave man finally lets the cobra loose in the pit, and as it slithers around him, perking up its head, opening its hood while it lurches and spits, the crowd begins to realize the man intends to catch the deadly beast with his *bare hands!*

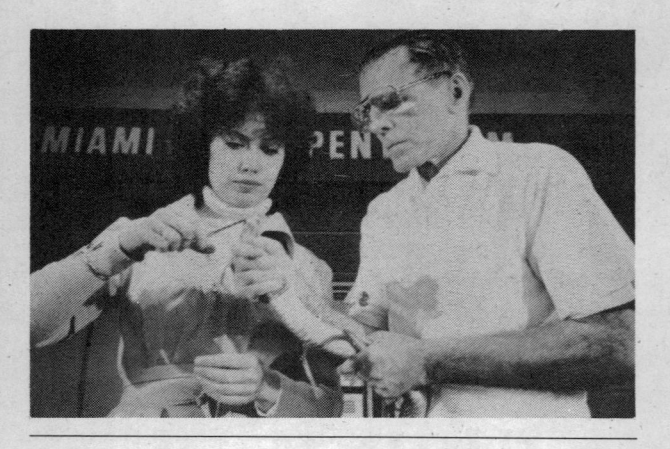

Incredibly, after several minutes made long by agonizing suspense, the man catches the cobra by its throat. It is furious, and this is just what the man wants. He takes the cobra to a beaker covered with a rubber top and allows the cobra to bite *that* ("Better the beaker than the man!" the crowd thinks). The cobra bites, ferociously, and an amber-colored liquid, a little like honey and with the same consistency, flows into the beaker.

But this is no honey. It's a deadly poison that kills most humans in a matter of minutes.

It's also the source of a life-giving treatment made from snake venom. That venom, in case you hadn't thought that far along, has to come from somewhere, and —since an angry snake provides better venom— this is the way Bill Haast gets it. He is the man in the pit, risking his life in the pit every day in order to get snake venom for the good of others. He has performed this unbelievable feat of venom extraction thousands and thousands of times.

THAT'S INCREDIBLE!

Bill Haast displays with pride the part of the Serpenterium never seen by the tourists—whose money, paid at the gate, supports what goes on here—that is, the spotless laboratory, filled with sophisticated equipment. Haast estimates that about $1 million has been invested in the laboratory alone.

"It is unquestionably the most sophisticated, largest, and advanced chromotology lab in the world," he says. "In this laboratory we separate the proteins and the enzymes from the venom which we collect and put into a product which we call Pro-Venom."

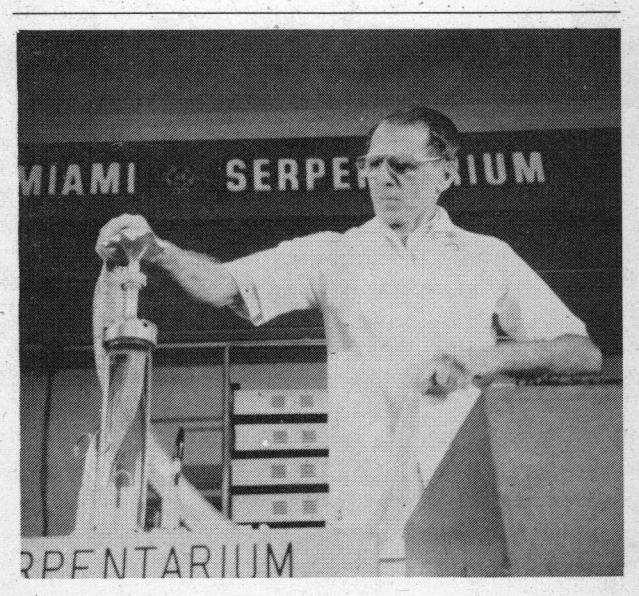

That amber venom, which Haast talks about so easily—now selling at about $50 per gram on the commercial market, making it about as valuable as gold—is immediately freeze-dried under the strictest scientific conditions. Dried this way, it can be kept almost indefinitely, to be shipped or kept right where it is for use anytime, anywhere.

Not that Haast has ever taken advantage of the hot product he concocts at the Serpenterium, mind you. Haast doesn't now, nor has he ever, charged for venom used in medical treatment, and at the Sheppard Clinic the entire course of treatment costs only $50—barely enough to cover the cost of the needles and syringes. No, Bill Haast has never been in it "for the money." He does what he does because he sincerely believes snake venom can be used for good purposes.

He's always been interested in snakes and their venom. His job in the 1940's as an airlines flight engineer allowed him to pursue his interest, and he traveled the world talking to experts and collecting snakes. Grounded at his own request in 1946, he worked as an aviation mechanic and at the same time began working on the Serpenterium, which he opened to the public two years later.

No dummy, Haast knew he was bound to be bitten eventually, so he began a slow process of making himself immune to snake venom. He did this by diluting cobra venom and injecting himself with it. Using a salt solution in which the venom was diluted 1000 times, he injected 1/100 cubic centimeter, and gradually increased the doses. He has been bitten many times, and has had a few close calls, but his blood is now so full of venom antibodies that he has always pulled through. His blood is now even thought to be a cure for deadly snakebite: Haast has often flown long distances to allow his blood to be transferred into the bodies of others

THAT'S INCREDIBLE!

in danger of death from snakebite, and at least twenty people are still alive because of him. Bill never charges for this gift of life, and even pays his own travel expenses.

At the Sheppard Clinic, snake venom is in ever-increasing demand. Whether or not it truly does any good has yet to be proved or disproved. But to some of those victims of multiple sclerosis or arthritis, it might offer at least a hope.

Ben Sheppard, director and founder of the clinic and himself a satisfied user of the venom, knows from his own experience and believes very strongly that the venom can work.

"This is the only place where these people can get snake venom," says Dr. Sheppard. "Even if we offer only a sixty-percent chance of success, that's more than anyone else is offering. And we offer it not as a cure, because it won't cure. But snake venom will certainly alleviate the symptoms and help in remission."

That simple reason is enough to bring the throng of hopefuls who daily gather around the clinic in hopes of taking part in its treatment. Only further research will prove whether that reason is valid or just another pipe-dream.

Either way, Bill Haast continues to produce and sell over two kilograms of dried venom every year. That may not sound like much, but that two kilos of venom represents about 36,000 venom extractions by Haast, from poisonous snakes native to twenty-one different countries. That many extractions mean too much danger to even think about, but for Bill Haast it's just all in a day's work. He almost makes it look easy.

Watch him do an extraction from a king cobra,

for instance, the only animal in the world (other than the human animal) that can kill an elephant.

He takes the snake, which weighs about fifteen pounds, out of its basket by using a long pole with a hook on the end of it, then letting the snake slither off the hook and onto the floor. The snake, of course, tries instantly to escape (as Bill's wife, Clarita, explains, "The snake doesn't want to be

THAT'S INCREDIBLE!

caught"), but Bill brings it back with the hook-ended pole.

What would happen if Bill weren't still taking his monthly booster shots, a mixture of twenty-eight snake venoms, and were no longer immune to bites? "Well, I'd die," Bill says calmly, knowing what would happen because he's been there himself— about forty times, in fact. "You go into respiratory

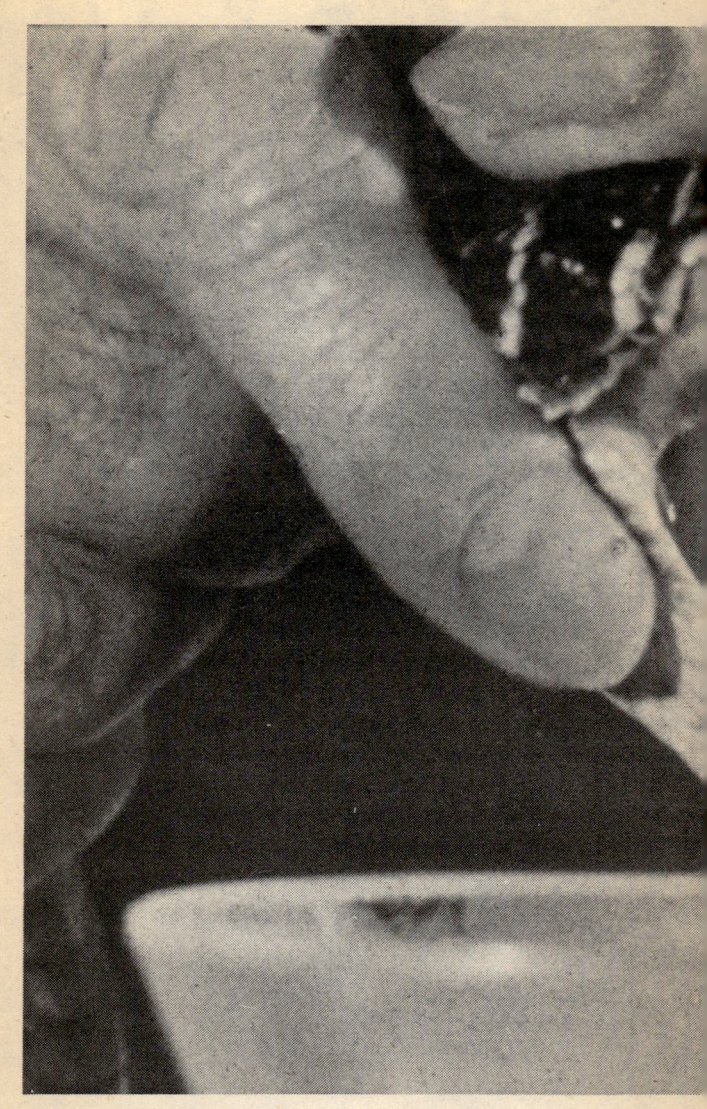

THAT'S INCREDIBLE!

25

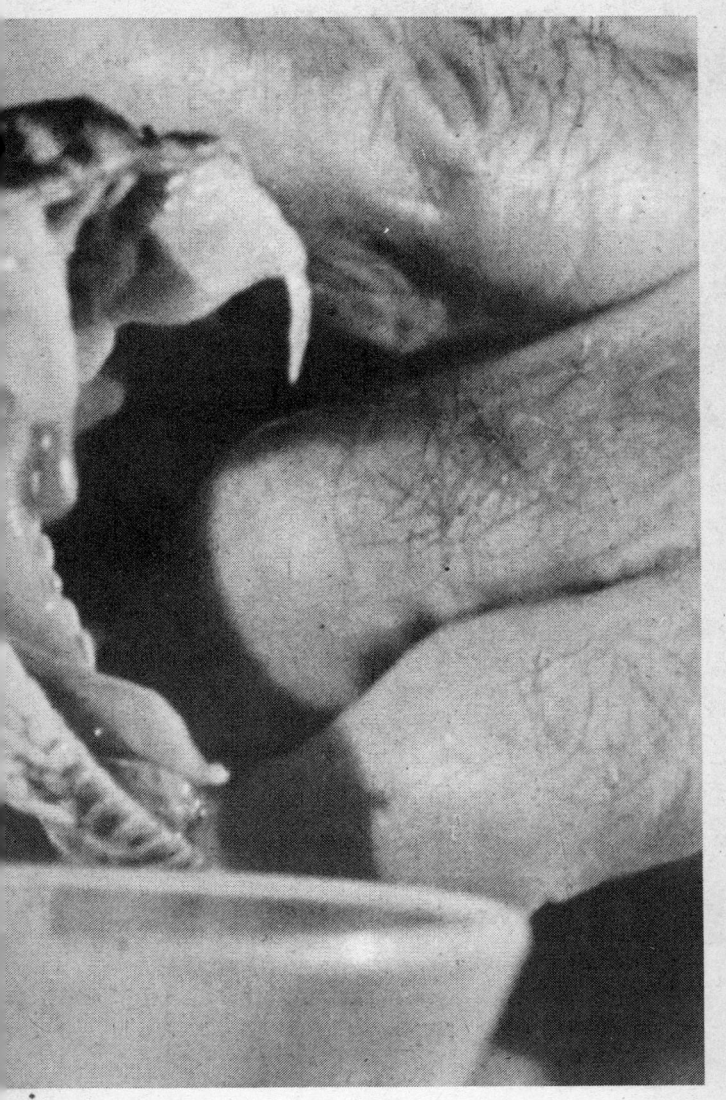

failure soon after the bite. You'd become very unstable, almost as if you were drunk. Then your body becomes very flaccid, then your respiratory system would become involved and just stop abruptly. And that would be it." It's all so simple, yet so deadly.

But Bill, as the only human being ever to survive the bite of the super-dangerous blue krait, is no normal man, and so he can bravely stare straight into the cold eyes of the king cobra and know he hasn't too much to fear.

The snake becomes angry, rears its head and spreads its hood, hissing and darting. It spreads its hood in an attempt to look larger and more terrifying to the person attacking it, but Bill is more respectful than terrified, so the hood does no good.

Bill has to be fast on his feet, agile as a cat to catch this fourteen-foot-long reptile. He weaves from side to side, using his arms like a gymnast on a balance-beam, hoping to attract the snake's attention with one hand so he can grab it around the neck with the other. But the snake has peripheral vision and can see 212 degrees, and one attempt after another to catch the snake fails. Even the failures are frightening to the observer, because the snake moves to strike each time he sees Bill's approaching hand, and it's hard to remember that Bill would survive the bite if the snake did manage to sink its impressive fangs into Bill's arm.

Then, in an instant, Bill's arm moves like a flash and he catches the snake at a point just below its head!

The snake thrashes, opening its jaws unbelievably wide, still hoping to get free and strike out at its attacker. Bill knows what comes next, and he's not

THAT'S INCREDIBLE!

about to waste a single drop.

Bill quickly carries the angry snake to a covered beaker and presses its fangs down into the rubber top. The snake bites eagerly, over and over again, and the venom begins to flow, oozing through the holes and into the beaker. He's biting in self-defense, thinking the rubber is part of the creature that was threatening him, and the venom continues to flow.

"To be bitten by this snake," explains Clarita Haast, standing not far away and breathing a little easier now that the beast is at bay, "is like being bitten by three to five cobras at one time. That's why he's the king. King cobras are like living syringes loaded with poison, moving through the jungle and shooting a little bit into everything that angers or frightens them."

The thought is a frightening one. But if it's true that snake venom can be used to ease the suffering of humans, and even animals, then perhaps poisonous snakes are not all bad.

On the chance that that *is* true, Bill Haast continues to do what seems to be his "act" at the Serpenterium in Miami, Florida, catching deadly snakes and harvesting their venom, placing himself in danger so that others may live without suffering.

2 / CAR JUMPER!

You're standing on a parking lot. You're wearing a white tee-shirt and loose-fitting blue sweat pants that are easy to move in. Soon you start limbering up, stretching, and doing cartwheels.

Several hundred yards from you a red Lotus switches on its powerful engine. You can hear it rumble. It pulls away and roars off to the far end of the parking lot.

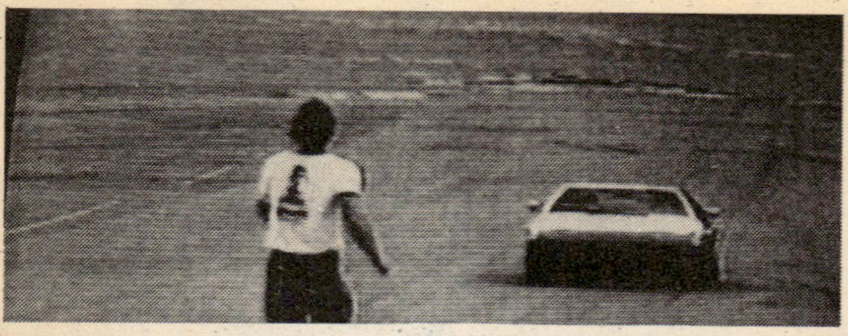

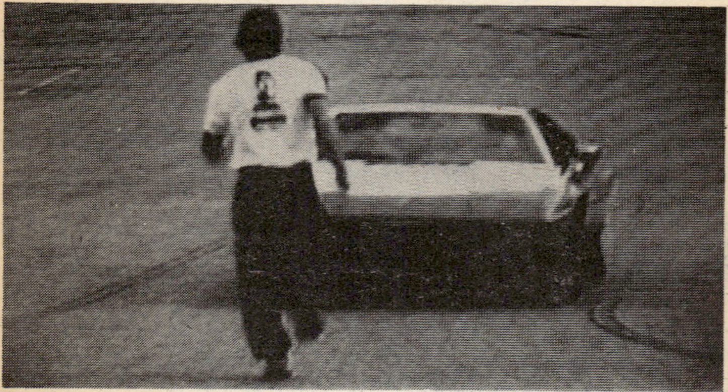

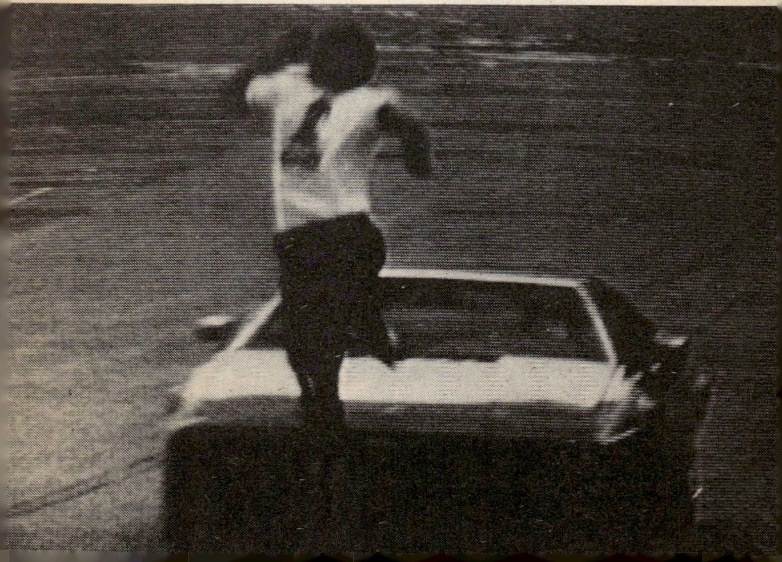

Then it slows, turns, and points itself straight at you. And then it begins to move. First slowly, then faster, ever faster, and you can hear each gear move upward as the Lotus's speed increases. The driver has aimed the Lotus right at you.

You're looking at the car, concentrating, concentrating. The driver has increased his speed to 70 miles per hour. You continue to stand directly in its path.

Then the Lotus is just a few yards—fractions of a second—away from you. You begin to run toward it. Are you

A. crazy;
B. ready to die; or
C. Steve Lewis?

The answer, of course, is Steve Lewis. Steve, a

skilled and highly trained athlete who just happens to be Southern California's Middleweight Kick-Boxing Champion, watches the Lotus's approach carefully (after all, his life depends on it). When it has reached just the right spot, at just the right speed, Steve runs just the right number of steps toward it. He then leaps high in the air—just high enough for the low-slung red Lotus to pass underneath him.

Incredible? You bet it is. And so unbelievably dangerous that only a highly trained athlete like Steve would *even dream* of trying it.

And even he thinks twice about it, although he's done it many times. The first time he did it—at Caesar's Palace in Las Vegas, Nevada—he tried car jumping with what might be called a complete lack of success: he broke his neck in two places, not to mention his left ankle.

How does an athlete like Steve go about training

THAT'S INCREDIBLE!

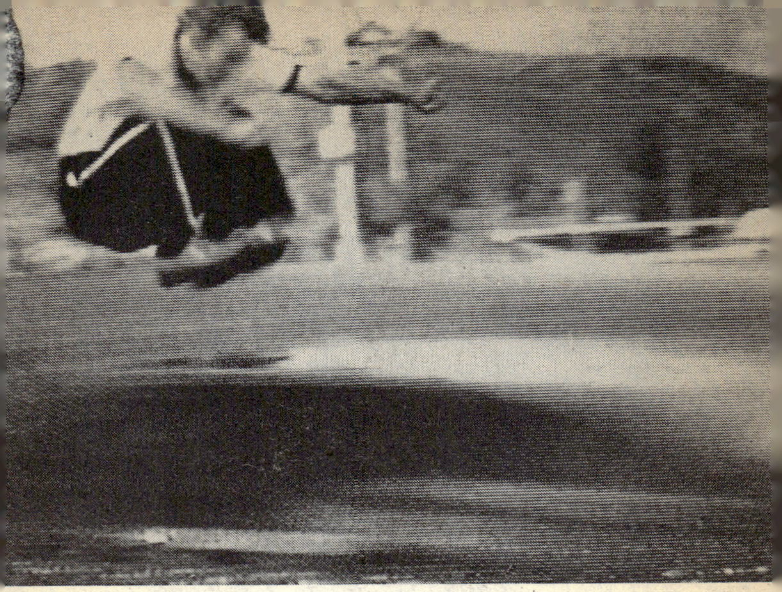

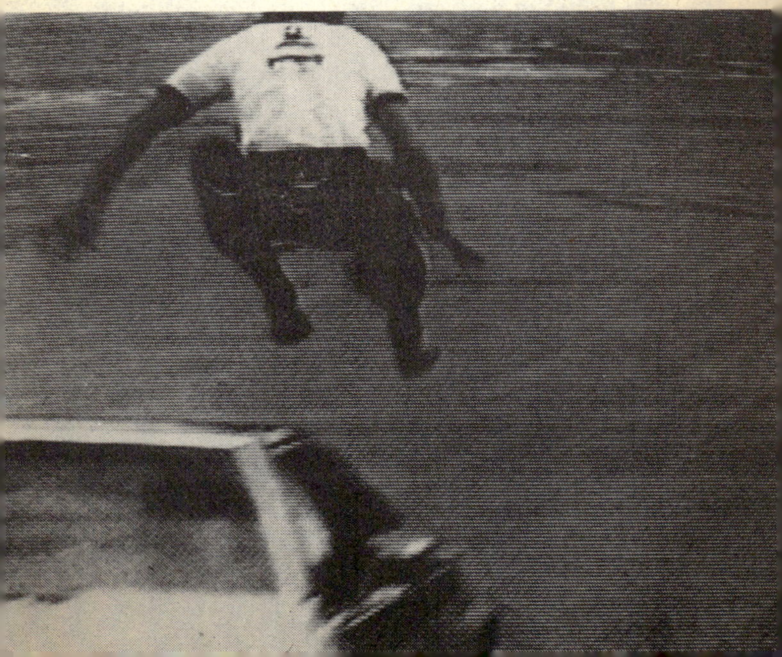

for such a super-dangerous stunt?

The initial answer, of course, is *very carefully*. He uses two cars with two drivers. The cars approach him from the right, and they follow each other in a circle. As one approaches, Steve jumps, and as he does so a camera records the action, giving Steve an opportunity later to watch his height, timing, and technique. At a set interval, the second car will approach him, Steve jumps over it, and the two cars continue to circle, one after another.

"For the main jump, though," Steve laughs, with just a touch of nervousness, "I use the same driver. Don't want to switch that." Is that the same thing as the old saying about not changing horses in midstream?

Big, blond, glowing, and muscular, Steve knows how dangerous his stunt is and makes no macho jokes that might mislead anyone about how difficult it is to jump over a moving car—especially one going 70 miles per hour.

"Aren't you frightened when a car's coming at

THAT'S INCREDIBLE!

you at that kind of speed?" Steve was once asked. "Don't you panic?"

Steve smiles, and shakes his head. "There's no time to be frightened," he says. Now that's *really* incredible!

3 STRUCK BY LIGHTNING!

(EIGHT TIMES LUCKY)

He doesn't look a bit different from anybody else. As a matter of fact, he probably looks exactly like someone you know, your Uncle Dave or your grandfather, maybe. He's not young, and he's got white hair—not much of it, though—and possibly he doesn't move as quickly as he used to.

But don't be mistaken. He's a park ranger in Virginia's Shenandoah National Park, and he's one of the most unusual people you've ever met. Why?

Because of what happened to him eight times, of course.

The first time it happened he was sitting in a large, empty outbuilding. "I was right here in this building," he says, "sitting in this chair. It must have come in through the ceiling. It knocked me over, chair and all."

The second time, he was sitting by a creek, in a meadow bordered by thick woods. "I was walking along here, and by golly, it got me right on the hip and it came out by my big toe."

The third time he was sitting on a rock, fishing. "The darn thing came along and hit me on the head and I fell off into the creek."

The fourth time, he was strolling through the forest. "I was walking this trail, and all of a sudden it came and got me from behind on the right shoulder and rolled me over."

The fifth time, he was by his trailer. What could it do to him there? "I had just walked out of the trailer, and was standing nearby when it came down and hit me in the shoulder and it rolled me over and over on the ground."

The sixth time? "I was riding along the road and it came through the window and it got me on the right side of the head and I was knocked unconscious."

And the seventh and eighth times? "I was just standing, and it got me. Lifted me right off the ground. Once it knocked my right shoe off!"

What in the world is it, this thing that has a thing about attacking one unsuspecting park ranger? Is it Bigfoot, or maybe a bear? Nope.

"I have been struck by lightning eight times,"

THAT'S INCREDIBLE!

says Park Ranger Roy Sullivan, and although he looks like he might be kidding, you know he's not.

One question leaps instantly to mind. Probably everyone he tells his incredible story to asks him the same question, so he answers it briefly. What, everyone wants to know, does it feel like to be struck by lightning?

"It's awful hot each time," replies Roy, a hint of laughter echoing in his soft Southern drawl. Everyone's gotten a small shock, from a plug for example, of maybe 110 volts or maybe as many as 240 volts, but being struck by lightning is "maybe thousands of times hotter."

Roy Sullivan has no explanation for why lightning comes looking for him when it needs a place to strike. Evidently science has been unable to provide a reason either, so Roy simply says, "I think there must be a chemical or a metal in my body that attracts lightning."

There sure must be!

But seeing is believing. Most people who are struck by lightning are either seriously injured or die as a result. It's easy to say it's happened to you eight times, but there's one problem: Roy's still alive. Roy has proof to back up his claim, and he's more than happy to show it. As a matter of fact, he gets a tremendous kick out of the wondering look that comes over the faces of those Doubting Thomases when he pulls out his hat and his watch.

The hat is nothing extra. He holds it up, and there's nothing odd about it—the kind of light-brown ranger's hat Smokey the Bear always wears.

But then he turns the hat slightly, and the hole

THAT'S INCREDIBLE!

comes into view, a puncture in the side of the dome, surrounded by burned, smoke-stained material. "This happened the sixth time," he says. "See, the lightning came down this time and struck me on the head and my hat went off. It went down my right side and it set my underclothes on fire. Then it raised me off the ground, knocked my right shoe off and set my sock on fire. I was cookin' fast."

Wait a second. Did he say the lightning set his *underwear* on fire? Yes, he did, and it did the same thing on another occasion too. That dismays him a little: the underwear was too burned up to use as evidence. But in the midst of his disappointment he smiles and says, "Now if you say that's not hot, I'd like to know what is."

He does, however, have another item of proof. And it's his watch.

The watch. Now that was the very first time Roy was struck by lightning, way back in 1942. "I had this watch in my pocket," he says, "and I was walking under the telephone line. That lightning bolt burned a hole in this side of the watch, and then it came out on the other side."

He holds up the watch, and there are the holes, each ringed with smoke singes. It really was struck by lightning! Roy shakes it, and a faint clatter is heard. "This was a ninety-eight-cent watch, and it's ruined. Melted the works clean together." He looks at the watch lovingly, as at a deeply hurt friend. "It was a beautiful watch, a good watch." But from the looks of it, there's not a prayer of it's ever running again.

The watch died, but Roy Sullivan survived. And that's another miracle Roy can't explain. He mentions the sixth strike again. "I was going along, driving a government vehicle, and I had each window down about six inches. Lightning struck two trees on the right side of the road, bounced off, came through the car, and hit me on the right side of the head. Then it went on through and killed another tree on the left side of the road. All three trees died, and I survived."

There's an obvious joke people might make when he says that, something about Roy Sullivan's head being thicker than wood. But Roy's bright as a silver dollar; he's thought a lot about what's happening to him, not that his thinking has helped him explain why lightning follows him around. But he has developed a standard operating procedure for

THAT'S INCREDIBLE!

any time rain begins to fall.

"If it's thundering and there's lightning and I'm at home, we go inside—that's my family and me—and I put my family in the living room. I sit away from the rest of 'em, in the dining room."

That, he hopes, will protect his family from lightning when he's around.

After Roy Sullivan has spent so much time answering questions about his life and luck with lightning, it's only natural to ask him if he has any questions of his own.

Not really, he says.

But then he raises his eyes to Heaven, and asks, "Why me?"

4 PAINLESS DENTIST

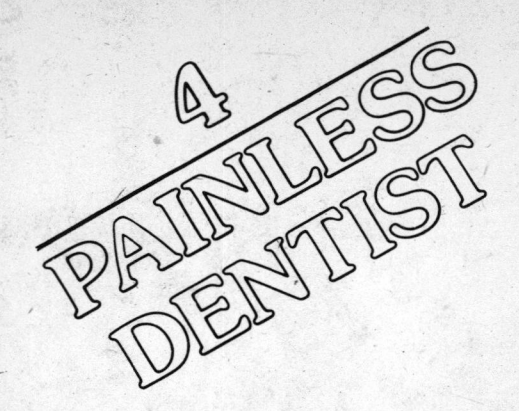

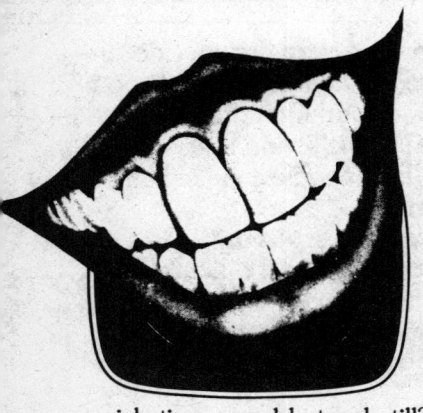

What is it that you dread most in the world? Is it final examinations, maybe, or—if you're a bit older than that—is it the idea of paying taxes that makes you wish time would stand still?

Well, be honest with yourself for a second while you ask yourself this question: What kind of score, on a dread scale of one to ten, does going to the dentist get?

45

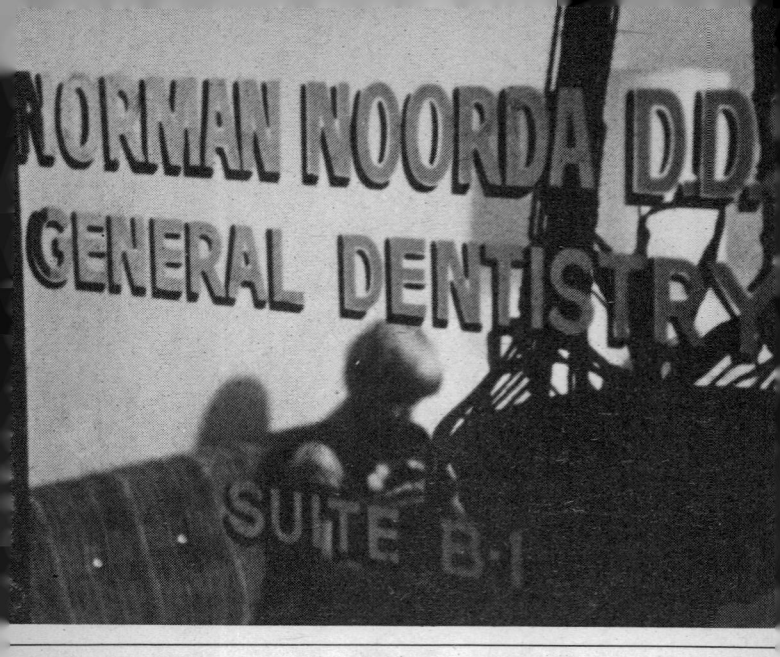

If you're like most people, you'd rather do almost anything than face the dentist. Probably you flinch every time you hear workmen drilling pavement in the street, because the sound is just a little too similar for comfort. Few people can help associating drilling with pain.

If you're still cavity-prone, or if your kids are, there's good news about going to the dentist, because somewhere out in the wild West there's a dentist who's made the agony of dental drilling a thing of the past—for about a third of his patients, anyway.

The dentist's name is Dr. Norman Noorda, and in his Las Vegas, Nevada, practice, he's pioneering an incredible "new" technique in painless dentistry. His method involves an extraordinary tool: a very ordinary household clothespin.

THAT'S INCREDIBLE!

And he's not kidding.

"We have found, obviously, that we can do better when we have a good doctor-patient rapport," says Dr. Noorda, "and for young patients—especially many from eight to twelve or fourteen, those young patients are generally more afraid of the needle injection."

This is probably no surprise to *anyone* who's seen that oversized, shiny-silver syringe coming at them.

"The first suggestion that they can get their teeth fixed without a shot is heaven on earth to them."

That kind of news would come as a welcomed relief to dental patients the world over, but—where does that clothespin come in?

We're getting to that.

Take young Glenn Cichoski, for instance, one of

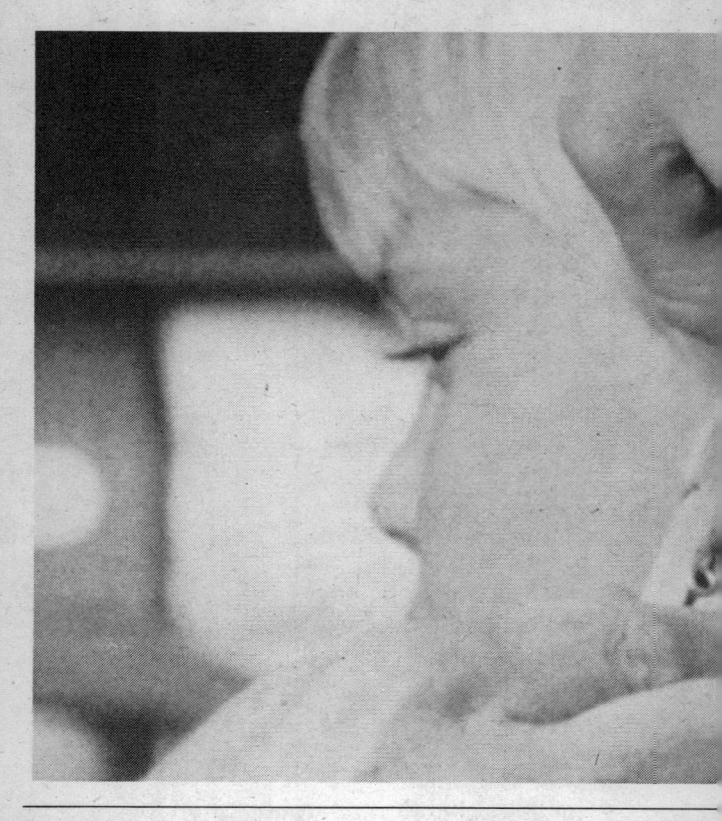

the doctor's patients, who candidly admits, "The first time I came to the dentist I was scared, but now it's really fun!"

Dr. Noorda is happy to explain the incredible change in Glenn's attitude. "Glenn had a hard time accepting the anesthetic without a shot. But when we showed him we were able to fix his teeth without the needle, he became a very good patient."

And then, as Glenn clambers into the much-

THAT'S INCREDIBLE!

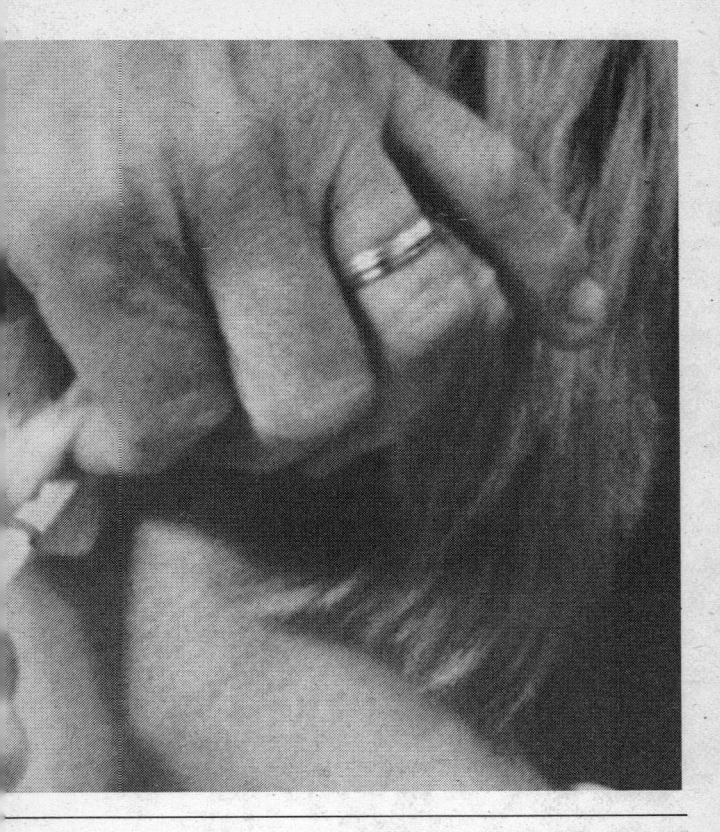

dreaded chair, gets comfortable, and allows Dr. Noorda's assistant to tuck the bib under his chin, the demonstration begins.

Taking a piece of cotton from a box, Dr. Noorda reaches across Glenn's chest and wraps a wad of cotton around Glenn's left earlobe. Then he uses a clothespin—just a common, ordinary clothespin—to hold the cotton in place.

"Does that hurt?" Dr. Noorda asks Glenn.

"Nope," Glenn replies, shaking his head.

"Then let's get to work," the doctor says. Glenn nods, and the peaceful look on his face tells you this little guy fears none of what's about to happen.

Dr. Noorda takes the drill from its hook overhead, deftly fits in the bit he'll need to use, and then — hunching over Glenn to get a better view — he begins to drill.

And he drills. And drills. And drills.

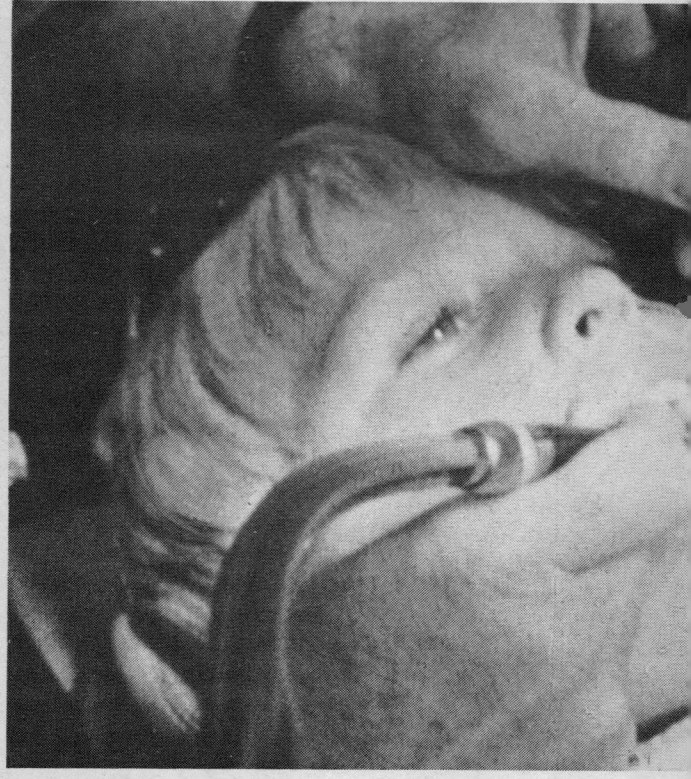

THAT'S INCREDIBLE!

Nine-year-old Glenn Cichoski doesn't move a muscle. He doesn't squirm or try to pull away from the dentist.

"How're we doing, Glenn?" the doctor asks, just to make sure. No method is goof-proof, after all!

"Fine," comes the garbled reply.

"Doesn't hurt? All righty..." Dr. Noorda continues his drilling.

The clothespin and the cotton are absolutely the

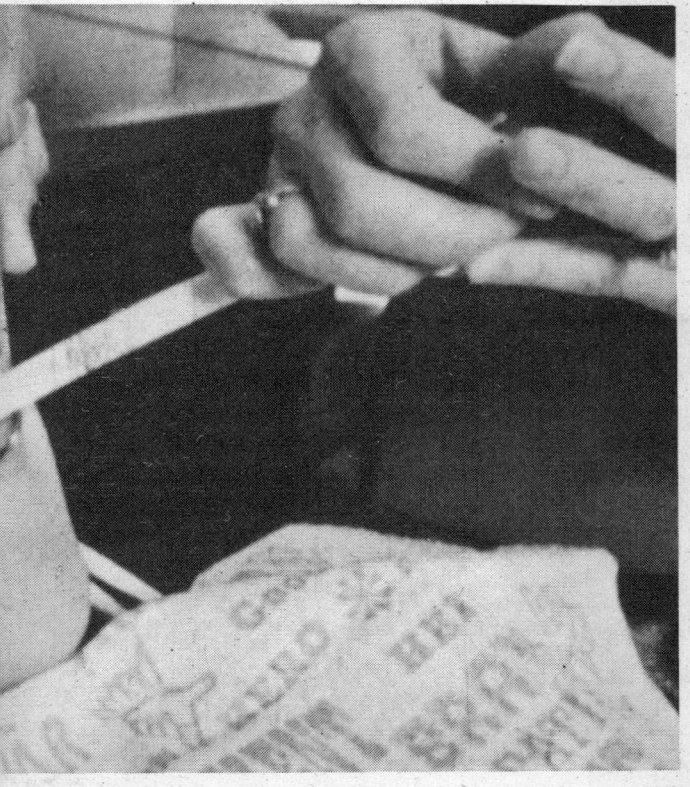

51

only painkillers that Dr. Noorda is using. Amazingly, Glenn isn't suffering the slightest bit of pain. Eventually the doctor finishes, and we've seen what might have seemed to be impossible: without the use of Novocaine or laughing gas, all pain has been removed from the dental process!

"What you've just seen," explains Dr. Noorda, "is acupressure for anesthetic in place of a shot or needle." He turns to Glenn. "That was a lot more comfortable than anesthetic from a needle, wasn't it?"

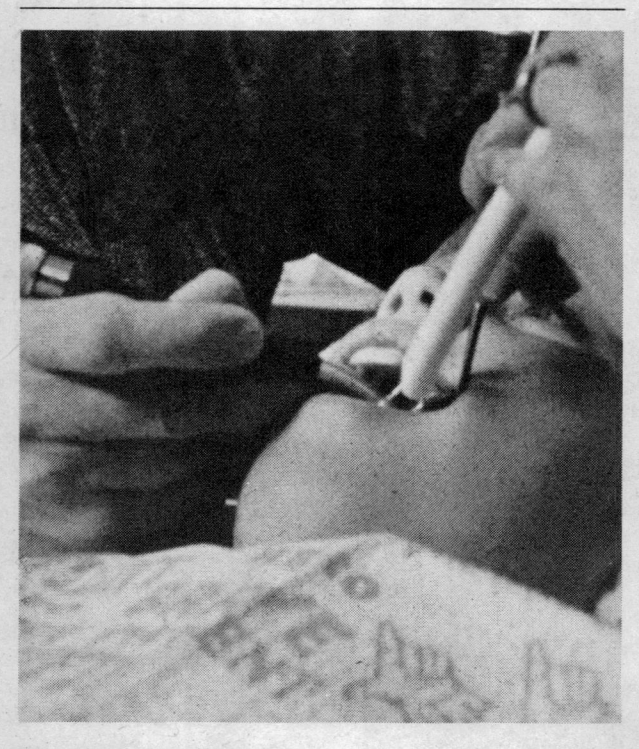

THAT'S INCREDIBLE!

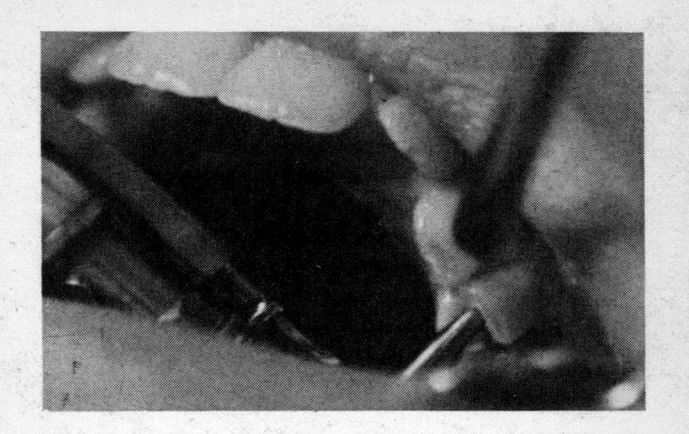

Glenn nods.

"Didn't hurt at all?"

This little man of a few words shakes his head, No.

"What we've done is, by placing that clothespin right in the center of the earlobe, we have actually created anesthesia in the mouth," he continues. "Now, it doesn't work on everybody, but on the patients who want it, it works fine. And Glenn here has been one of our best patients today—never had anything but the clothespin."

With that, he removes the clothespin and cotton, and Glenn gets down, having enjoyed one of the world's least-frightening trips to the dentist.

Dr. Noorda began using this amazing anesthetic in September, 1979, after hearing a lecture on acupuncture. He admits the whole thing may sound like hogwash, but it's hard to dismiss the kind of results this particular brand of hogwash brings.

He uses the earlobe because it's convenient, but actually the heel and the knee would work just as well. All three are main painkilling points in the body. Perhaps he felt more confident about using the earlobe because one of his patients has an amputated earlobe, and that side of his face is permanently numb.

In any case, Dr. Noorda felt strongly that this form of anesthetic had great promise, and eventually he began to experiment with the method. He found the clothespin stopped the patient from feeling any pain.

"Perhaps it works because the patient is concentrating on the pain in his ear," the doctor says with a warm laugh.

Gradually, by winning over his patients—one by one—to the idea of giving this strange new treatment a try, Dr. Noorda turned almost 35 percent of his patients into clothespin devotees. More are coming over to the drug-free, fear-free side all the time, but Dr. Noorda insists on using other anesthetics when he feels they are necessary. Generally he uses the clothespin method for fillings and cappings; major operations are something else again.

Once, however, he was forced to break his own rule when a young boy came to him, needing a particularly tricky and painful piece of dental work. The doctor decided to use an injected anesthetic, but the boy was terrified of needles and wouldn't allow the shot. A trifle reluctantly, Dr. Noorda fell back on his clothespin method, and the boy never even whimpered while the work was being done. He's now one of the doctor's happy and satisfied regular patients.

Another young patient, Marie Delespinasse, has only good words to say for Dr. Noorda and his clothespin. She'd resisted going to the dentist because "all my friends told me it hurts and I didn't want to have a big needle." The twelve-year-old adds, a little sheepishly, "it felt silly with a clothespin on my ear, but the drilling didn't hurt a bit."

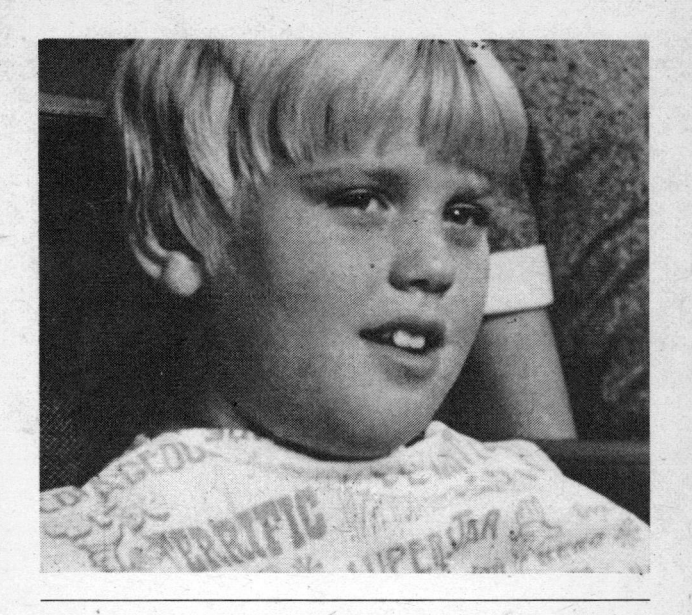

Will Dr. Norman Noorda's clothespin take the dental world by storm, turn that every-six-months visit to the dentist into what it's never been before—a pleasant experience instead of a much-dreaded hour of pain to put off just as long as possible?

Sometimes the medical world looks down on such simple improvements. But maybe, just maybe, some dentists—yours, perhaps?—will come around to Dr. Noorda's thinking. But if they don't, there are still those lucky patients in Las Vegas, who don't lose their smiles when they enter the doctor's office. They just leave with prettier ones.

5
BEAT THE CHICKEN!

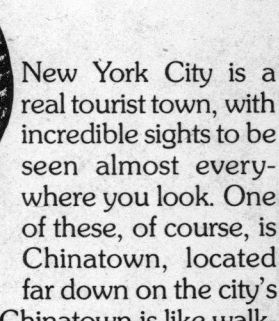

New York City is a real tourist town, with incredible sights to be seen almost everywhere you look. One of these, of course, is Chinatown, located far down on the city's east side. Strolling through Chinatown is like walking into another world: everyone, as far as the eye can see, is an Oriental, many dressed in traditional Chinese clothing; the food is the best Chinese cuisine on the East Coast; dragons loom from signs

THAT'S INCREDIBLE!

and—on special days—spectacular parades.

There's always something to do in Chinatown, even if all you can afford to do is walk. No telling what you might see. As a matter of fact, if you're walking down Mott Street and you peer into the arcade below the Chinese Museum, you'll see something you won't believe no matter how long you stand there trying to believe your eyes.

It's a chicken that plays tic-tac-toe. And wins. Almost always.

It's a real chicken, all right, behind a piece of plate glass. Drop a coin in the slot and the chicken will turn its attention toward a quick game of X's and O's—and the chicken always gets to go first. A light flashes, when the chicken's X appears on the board, to tell you it's your turn. And once you've made your move, the chicken ducks quickly into its thinking booth, takes its turn, and then it's up to you. Eventually you'll find you've lost, as a neon light flashes your humiliation to the world:

THE CHICKEN WINS.

There is, of course, a chance that the chicken *won't* win. Certainly even our fine feathered friends are not infallible, even the most capable of them. And if it's an off day for the chicken, you'll win a bag of fortune cookies. But don't wet your lips and head for the subway unless you're a good loser: that chicken plays a mean game of tic-tac-toe.

(By the way, the chicken switches off days with a more artistic bird that dances when properly paid off. So those more interested in culture than games of skill may want to come back for the chicken ballet.)

But enough fooling around. What's the story behind that glass? Who taught the chicken to play the most flawless game of tic-tac-toe in town?

Nobody, really, unless it was HAL9000. You see, the chicken is a mere pawn in a computer game. Play tic-tac-toe with the chicken, and you're in fact squaring off for a duel of wits with a machine programmed to win, so that you'll most often lose.

What you can't see is hurting you. Each time a quarter is dropped in the slot, the computer is activated. It makes its first move, and it lights a small red light in the chicken's thinking-booth. The chicken, of course, has been taught—at great time and expense, no doubt—to peck at a tiny button under the light, and each time it does so it gets a reward. That button it presses lights an X on the playing board—in the space chosen by the computer. Given the first move, the chicken will always win. Or at least appear to.

The chicken was trained by the Animal Behavior School in Hot Springs, Arkansas, and sent to

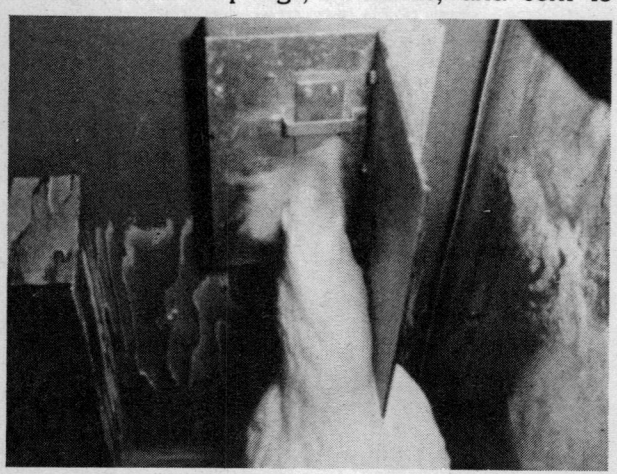

THAT'S INCREDIBLE!

Chinatown to frustrate the general population. The bird happens to be a female, and if anything ever puts her out of the tic-tac-toe racket she'll have to be replaced by another female: it seems males aren't smart enough.

Wondering why she gets a day off every other day? Seems overweight is a problem. All that rewarding puts too much meat on the chicken's bones, which causes a very-much-unwanted heart condition.

No matter how much people know about the trick, no matter how many times they're beaten, they still come back to take one more crack at beating the chicken. Children, of course, are her most avid opponents, standing there for hours at times trying for the elusive bag of fortune cookies.

One child, an almond-eyed, black-haired young thing of perhaps five years, however, finally gave up in disgust. Asked why, she sighed a little, shrugged a little, and said, "It's no fair. That chicken's too smart."

Smart, maybe. But she also gets the best advice in town.

6 / THE FIRE INSIDE

Not that it was a downright *dull* way to spend his day, but there was no way Don Gosnell could say any spectacular events made one day more memorable from the one that had come before or the one that would follow. That was until the morning of December 5, 1966, anyway.

Don Gosnell is a meter reader with the gas company that serves Coudersport, Pennsylvania, a sleepy, gingerbread sort of town where you'd hardly expect anything out-of-the-ordinary to happen. But it did. And Don Gosnell was the man who detected it first.

That morning, he was making his usual morning rounds on his usual route, checking meters. At about 9:05 he arrived at the home of Dr. John Bentley, and—as people in small towns will do—he simply opened the door, leaned in, and yelled "Gas man!" Nothing out of the ordinary; all according to custom.

But there was no answer to Don Gosnell's call, which was odd. He knew the doctor was usually at home this time of day, and he ventured inside, sensing something might not be quite right.

Closing the door behind him softly, shutting out the glare of the early sun and the scent of the clean morning air, he confirmed his suspicions: the house seemed to be full of a light blue smoke, and the smoke gave off a sickeningly sweet odor.

Don Gosnell decided to go downstairs first, check the meter, and get the first order of business out of the way. That done, he'd come back upstairs and investigate the smoke problem. He walked quietly through Dr. Bentley's house, knowing the route to the doctor's basement door as well as he knew the way to his own at home. The smoke, he found, was everywhere; instinctively he put his hand over his nose and mouth, but the smoke got in his eyes and the sickly, honey-sweet smell invaded his nose. He was glad to get to the basement door: perhaps the smoke had not seeped into the cellar.

Stooping as he walked down the cellar steps, Don Gosnell turned to read the meter, but before he could move close to it he noticed a pile of ashes

THAT'S INCREDIBLE!

on the floor.

Crossing to it, seeing no fire-related debris around it, Gosnell looked up. Sure enough, there was a hole, and around the hole stood tiny red embers. Gosnell nodded to himself, glad Dr. Bentley had managed to get out before he got hurt.

But then he got to thinking again. Why hadn't someone called the fire department—a neighbor, for instance, or the doctor himself from a nearby

65

phone booth? It made no sense. He himself had been in the house long enough for the fire trucks to report to the house.

And what about the smell? He'd never smelled anything quite like it before. The blue smoke was new to him, too.

Looking up through the hole, Gosnell recognized the doctor's study. He walked back upstairs, down the hall to the study, knocked gently—after all, you never know—and opened the door.

Looking in, he saw just a pile of ashes on the floor. Nothing really burned in the room, just this pile of ashes on the floor, right where the hole was, and—

Just hold on a minute here, said Don Gosnell to himself. The sweet smell was strongest here, but Gosnell could not cover his nose and look more closely at the ash at the same time.

There were shoes in the ashes, like the ones the doctor always wore. And there was fabric, and... Don Gosnell stood up, backed toward the study door. It was the doctor. It was all that was left of the doctor! Backing out of the study, Don Gosnell ran to the phone to call in his grisly discovery.

Just what happened to Dr. John Bentley? Don't ask that question if you're with a group of doctors—unless you want to listen to a lot of arguing.

What most probably happened to Dr. Bentley is what's come to be called Spontaneous Human Combustion, also called SHC, and what that means is that there are times when a human body—for no reason at all—will suddenly burst into flame and completely destroy itself, leaving just ashes and perhaps some bits of charred bone. SHC is totally different from "self-immolation," in which

THAT'S INCREDIBLE!

a person pours gasoline over himself, then sets himself alight. In SHC, the body has no help at all—no lighted cigarette or match—to help it along. Something in the body's chemistry just simply ignites. And *that's* probably what happened to Dr. John Bentley.

The facts of the Bentley tragedy reached Larry Arnold, a researcher and writer who's investigated similar incidents and has his own thoughts about SHC.

"Several things make Spontaneous Human Combustion very, very baffling," says Arnold. "The body is reduced entirely or almost completely, depending on the episode, literally to ashes. Very little anatomy is left in recognizable form.

"In a normal death by fire the body, even though it's severely damaged by the flames, remains intact and fully recognizable as the body of a human being. And, of course, the surrounding combustible objects are severely damaged by the flames as well.

"What characterizes a case of SHC, however, is that there is no damage to surrounding combustible objects. Additionally, rather than finding the unpleasant odor normally associated with burning

THAT'S INCREDIBLE!

flesh, one finds either no aroma at all or a sweet perfumelike scent in the room where the victim has died."

Dr. Bentley's death—if that's what it was—certainly meets the requirements of a case of SHC. Don Gosnell had been overpowered by the sweet smell. And as for the condition of the corpse, the body was so completely consumed by the intense heat that the total destruction couldn't have been done intentionally even if gasoline had been used!

Possibly most incredible is the fact that nothing else in the room was noticeably damaged. To cremate a body to the extent that Dr. Bentley's body was reduced to ashes, heat would have had to be kept at 2200 degrees Fahrenheit for three hours. Obviously, had that been the case at Dr. Bentley's house, the entire house would have gone up in flames. Obviously what happened to the doctor happened quickly, too quickly to melt the rubber tips on the doctor's walker, even too quickly to burn the shoes he was wearing, let alone the house in which he lived.

Four years after the doctor's ghastly death, the house was purchased by a new owner, who has lived in it for ten years without incident. He, too, is still baffled by what happened in his home in 1966, and he looks at the beams below the doctor's study in absolute amazement.

"The strangest thing, to me," he says, "is that the man could have been so consumed and yet there would have been so little damage to the structure here and to the rest of the house."

He points to the joists below the doctor's study, the joists above his head. "The fire apparently was all contained within a three-foot circle, and it burned this main joist, along with the two alongside it."

Dr. Michael Persinger has made an extensive study of the phenomenon of SHC.

"With respect to SHC," he begins in his scholarly way, "here again we have a bizarre event that appears to violate the basic assumptions of science.

"If we assume that there are a hundred cases in

the last two hundred years that are well documented, in North America and in Europe, and that there have been roughly five to six hundred million people in that time span, then we're talking about a phenomenon that's rarer than the rarest disease.

"One model that appears to fit the data is that the SHC phenomenon is not really a fire at all but rather a highly intense, highly localized electrical current that occurs within the body due to certain kinds of earth processes associated with earthquake phenomenon in the region."

(Larry Arnold, by the way, thinks there may be another name for what Dr. Persinger calls "electrical current," but we'll come back to that.)

Having reassured his listener by saying that SHC is so rare that there's absolutely no reason to fret that it might happen to you, Dr. Persinger admits that the file on Dr. John Bentley remains open. "We may never know exactly what happened to him, although clearly it was a case of Spontaneous Human Combustion."

Larry Arnold believes that, in order to get to the bottom of SHC, researchers need "cooperation from fire investigators and other individuals who have had contact with this kind of phenomenon. Such cooperation would help us to uncover clues that would enable us to understand how these things happen and thereby prevent others from experiencing this kind of flaming fate."

Arnold, of course, is no snob: he's fascinated by documented SHC cases that cause the death of the victim—and also by SHC cases in which the body bursts into flame *after* the body is already dead. He's aware of a number of such cases, and has done quite a bit of thinking on the subject of postmortem SHC.

There was, for instance, the case of fifty-year-old Betty Satlow of Hoquiam, Washington. She was found dead on the seat of her car on Friday, December 7, 1973, by her husband. She was probably intoxicated when she died, and the coroner blamed her death on carbon-monoxide poisoning, but he was reluctant to call the death either homicide or suidide.

Either way, Mrs. Satlow was prepared for a burial on Monday. But before she was removed from the mortuary, smoke was reported coming from the coffin. Firemen arrived and found the fire: inside the mortuary, inside a coffin, *inside* Mrs. Satlow!

No reason was ever found for the spontaneous blaze that consumed the body completely, right down to the waist. Was it SHC? Very probably that's just what it was.

THAT'S INCREDIBLE!

There was also the strange case of Glenn Burk Denny, age forty-six, of Algiers, Louisiana. On Thursday, September 18, 1952, firemen broke down the door of Denny's apartment and found him—and only him—a mass of flame in the middle of the floor.

"In all my experience," said one of the firemen, Lieutenant Louis Wattigny, "I never saw anything to beat this."

At first, foul play was investigated; after all, no source or reason could be found for the fire that had killed Denny. But then it was discovered that the fire had not been the cause of Denny's death: Glenn Burk Denny, who'd slashed both wrists and both ankles, was a suicide. His body had burst into flames either as he died or after he was dead!

Checking through the list of "combustible corpses," Larry Arnold noticed that many of them were either officially termed suicides who were later consumed by fire, or else police were tempted but reluctant to term the death a suicide.

This coincidence caused Arnold to check back into the research already done in an attempt to prove the existence of a human soul. One study had resulted in the conclusion that a body weighed twenty-one grams less just after death. Could that missing twenty-one grams represent the soul leaving the physical body? Perhaps.

Arnold also took note of the many interviews done with persons who, at some point in their lives, were pronounced dead—only to come back to life later. Their thoughts on death, their experiences while "dead," were incredibly similar, and thus some researchers were tempted to confirm the existence of some kind of afterlife.

A person who dies gradually, however, is quite different from one who dies a quick, violent death, or one who takes his or her own life. When death comes slowly, the "soul" prepares slowly for passage from the physical body into whatever "afterlife" there may be. With a quick and violent death or a suicide, the body and "soul" are separated abruptly, unexpectedly, without preparation time. Generally the body is harmed in some way, and begins to deteriorate the instant the "soul" is gone.

Which prompted Larry Arnold to wonder: What happens if the soul leaves the body and realizes that suicide is a horrible mistake, something that shouldn't happen? What happens if the soul then attempts to sneak back into the physical body—instantly, hours later, even days later (as in the case of Mrs. Satlow)? Can it do that?

Perhaps not, reasons Arnold. If the soul is considered a kind of electrical current, and the physical body and its processes another kind of electrical current, then we have to assume that—while the body is alive—the soul and body will work together in some kind of electrical harmony.

But if the soul *leaves* the body, then the soul remains the same but the body will begin to change. If the soul then tries to sneak back into the body, they will no longer be able to work together in harmony. In fact they may short-circuit. Sparks may fly.

And then, perhaps, a fire may start.

Could this be the reason for the great number of SHC cases connected to suicides? Larry Arnold thinks the idea may not be completely crazy.

And if nothing else, it is at least some kind of explanation for the how's and why's of Spontaneous Human Combustion. No matter how far-fetched anyone's thoughts on SHC may seem, none can be totally dismissed. There are no facts in the matter of SHC, only a handful of documented cases. The phenomenon remains one of life's most incredible mysteries.

7 / LIFE ON MAN

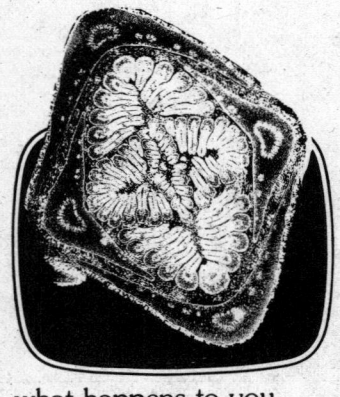

If you're like most people, you feel a little lonesome sometimes. You get to feeling down in the dumps, like nobody knows you're alive and nobody cares what happens to you.

There happens to be another viewpoint on that matter, and it might make you feel better or it might not, but the fact is that you could be shipwrecked alone on a desert island and still be constantly surrounded by literally millions of devoted friends.

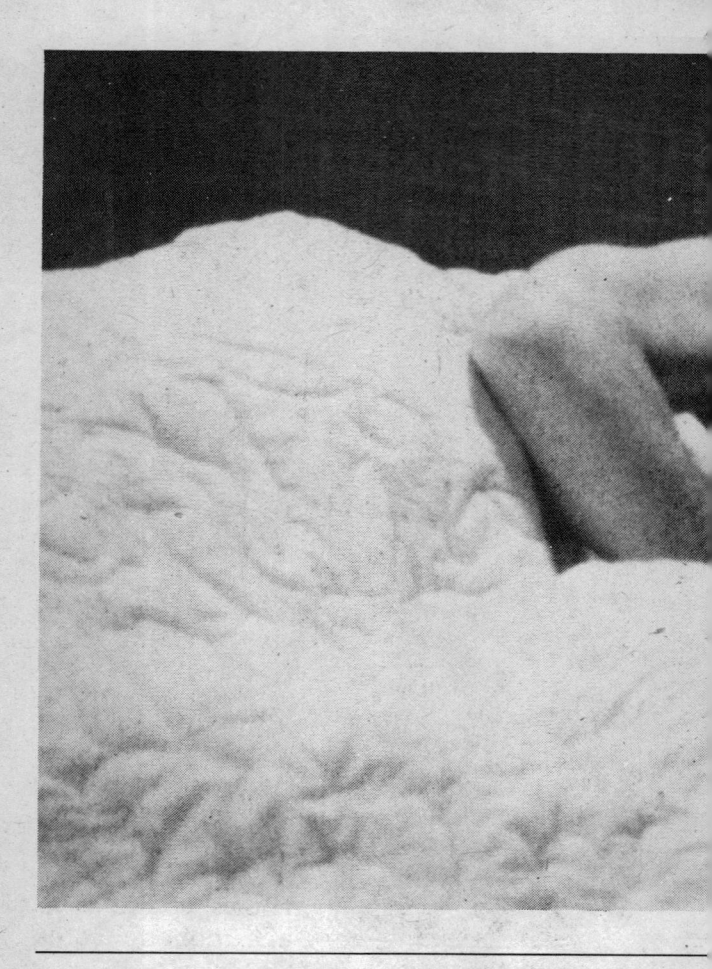

If this sounds a little strange to you, it's probably because you didn't know that, every single second of every single day of your life, you're at the center of a bizarre gallery of invisible life—too small for

THAT'S INCREDIBLE!

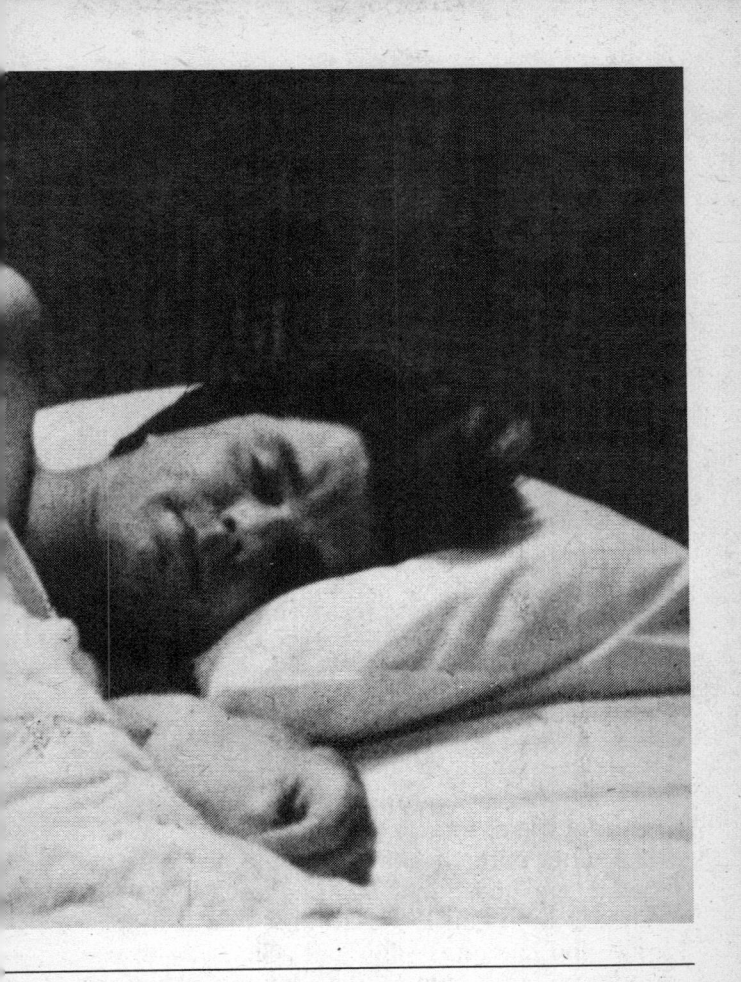

our naked eyes to see.

But oh, if you just had a high-powered microscope, the always-with-you buddies you could see!

Take your bed, just as an example. Maybe you're under the impression that you sleep alone.

Well, guess again.

In the sheets and blankets of nearly everyone's bed live colonies of microscopic dust mites. When photographed with an electron microscope, these little creatures look like alien beings from some far-distant world, but they're not, They're from right here on earth, and they're with us always. Countless unseen generations of these close companions live out their lives right under your very nose (especially if you happen to sleep on your stomach).

These dust mites may not be terribly attractive, but we're not likely to get rid of them. They depend on us for their very lives. Dust mites—and all their relatives and friends—feed primarily on the flakes of dead skin that our bodies constantly shed. What's dead to us is dinner to the population that inhabits our bedding.

Live skin, of course, offers a home for numerous other invisible creatures. For instance, in the roots of everyone's eyelashes live tiny mites called *Domodex folliculorem*. Scientists have never been able to explain what they're doing there, but the fact is that—whatever they're up to—they're not doing anyone any harm. Therefore nobody worries about them; they're just there.

But other parts of our bodies can easily be invaded by tiny guests that aren't as easy to live with.

There's the head louse, to take one example. He's a tiny creature—tiny, yet still visible to the naked eye—that, given half a chance, will happily take up permanent residence in your hair. Reluctant to be brushed off, he makes sure his stay is a long one by locking his powerful claws around a single strand of your hair.

Another unwelcome creature, the scabies mite,

THAT'S INCREDIBLE!

makes a comfortable home for himself by burrowing directly into the skin. This little beast is one of the hardest to get rid of, once he's pitched camp.

Those are a few of the mites and lice that are always anxious to give your body as their home address. But there are living organisms even smaller that are always with you.

Let's look closely at the skin on a man's face. Looking at the surface of his face—through a microscope, at high magnification—a strange picture becomes visible. The surface may look a lot like fields and hillsides as seen from a plane at high altitude, full of hills and ravines.

Moving closer and closer, the stubble of the beard begins to look like the stumps of giant trees on a rough, hilly terrain.

On every strand of that hair live tiny fungi. In their many forms, they populate most parts of our bodies—and all together they number in the millions.

On the moist, warm regions of our skin—on the neck, for instance—there's life in incredible abundance, in the form of bacteria. One of the simplest and smallest forms of life, they are constantly with us. They've lived on us for millions of years, and have established a permanent niche in the habitat of our skin.

Bacteria can grow and multiply at incredible rates. In fact, at any given time, there are as many bacteria living on one person's skin as there are people living on the earth.

For some people, that's a rather nightmarish thought.

As a matter of fact, some people may be getting itchy just reading about the millions of lives thriving in and around their very own bodies. Maybe they're feeling itchy enough to go jump in the shower, hoping to wash away some of the skin-bound population.

If one of those people is you, don't bother with the shower unless you really need or want one. Showering won't rid you of your millions of fellow travelers. As a matter of fact, the warmth of the water will actually cause that population of bacteria

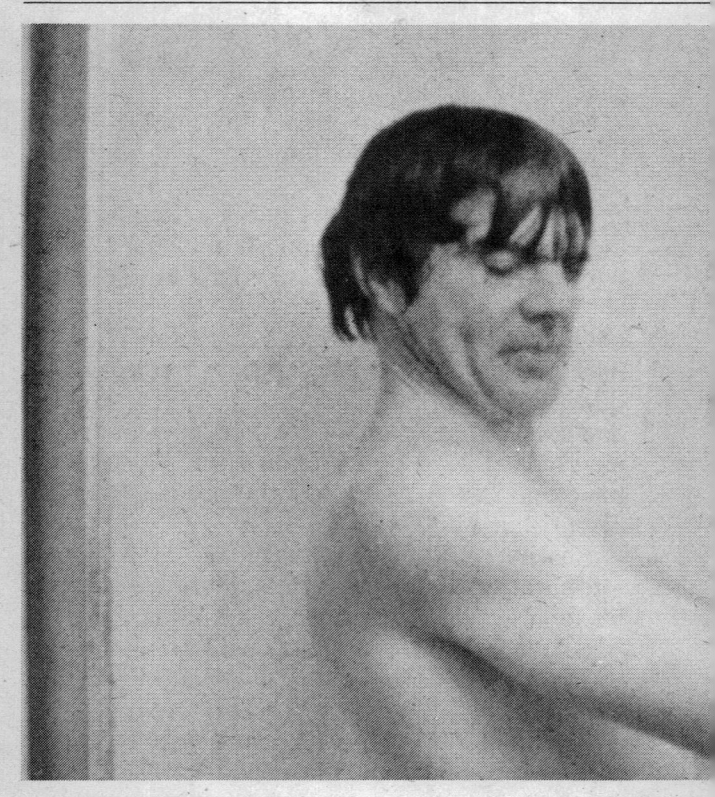

THAT'S INCREDIBLE!

to suddenly grow!

If it makes you feel any better, keep in mind that all your tiny guests are not hazardous to your health. In truth, they're healthy bacteria which repel other, far more damaging creatures that would gladly make our bodies their home.

So stop scratching and keep reading. And remember not to turn the page until *all* of you have finished reading it!

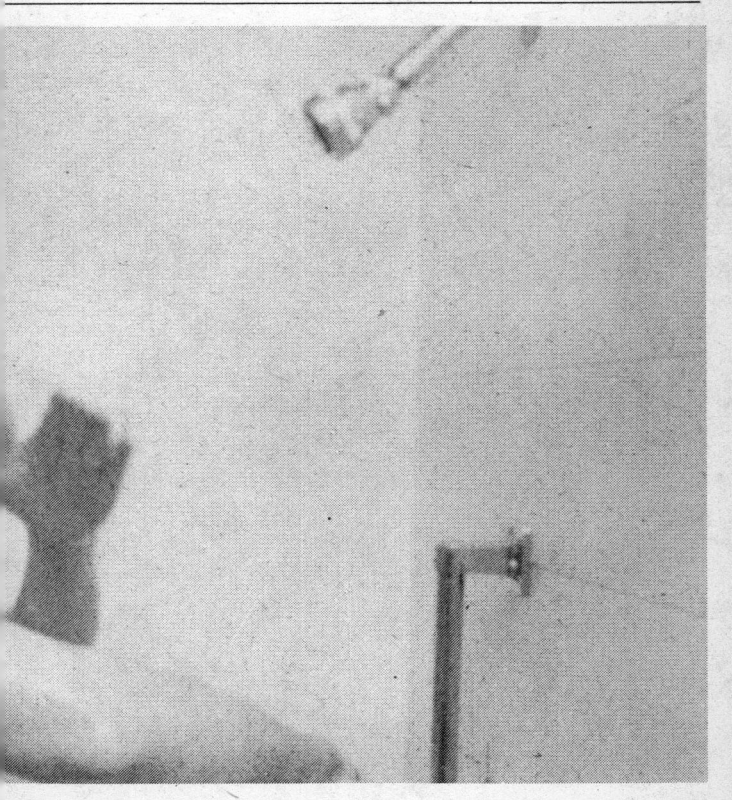

8 / THE HAUNTED HOUSE OF LOWELL, MASS.

Kathleen McGuire walked home from school that day, glad to be heading home but dreading the evening's homework, hoping there were still cookies in the jar and milk in the refrigerator. As she walked, she fished in her pocket for her house-key; always the first one home at the end of the day, she always had to let herself in. Her sisters, Eileen and Patricia, would still be on the way home, her parents still at

85

work—mother Marie at the hospital where she worked as a nurse, father Tom at his job with the Lowell School Department.

Kathleen turned the corner onto Beacon Street, and the 125-year-old house came into view. She and her family had lived in the trim white twelve-room house since 1969, and as she approached it, Kathleen looked up, as she always did—as if

THAT'S INCREDIBLE!

checking to see if the roof was still there, not that there was any danger of it going anywhere.

She stopped short, struck like a statue where she stood in the front yard, staring in wide-eyed terror into the unknown eyes that looked back at her from an upstairs window. No one was home. Her mother would have warned her if company had been expected. And how would they get in, without a key, if they were not expected? Kathleen stood for a fearful moment, staring into the eyes of the stranger—a tiny, almost childlike creature in a wide-brimmed hat—then turned on her heels, dropped her books, and ran.

Before she realized it, she'd run in the door of her best friend's house, the back door that opened into the kitchen. Her friend wasn't there, but her best friend's mother was already busy making supper. She turned, startled, when Kathleen entered abruptly.

"Why, Kathleen McGuire," she said, "you almost scared me to death. Why—" She saw Kathleen's terrified expression, and checked her impulse to scold. "What's the matter, honey? You look like you've seen a ghost. Sit down and tell me what's wrong."

Kathleen stopped, sat, and caught her breath. "There's somebody in our house, Mrs. Reid," she said. "I don't know who it is. I never saw him before."

"Was your mom looking for company?" Mrs. Reid asked, wiping her hands on her apron, lowering the flame under the pot on the stove.

"No ma'am," said Kathleen. "She'd have told me. I'd have to let them in. And I never saw this person in my life, Mrs. Reid. He looks like a little boy, like he got lost and came to our house by mistake. But how would he get in without a key?"

"Could be all kinds of reasons for that," said Mrs. Reid. "Maybe a window open, or you know how sometimes people forget to lock the back door . . ." The rebuke was a gentle one: locking the back door was something Kathleen sometimes forgot to do. Mrs. Reid thought a minute, then walked to the

THAT'S INCREDIBLE!

bottom of the staircase that led to her two son's bedrooms.

"John! Evan!" she called. "Put your shoes on, I've got something for you to do!"

Mrs. Reid's two college-bound sons walked Kathleen home again, and after she unlocked the door they made a systematic check of the house, room by room, as Kathleen walked fearfully behind them. When they'd checked the attic, and had looked the whole house over without finding anything or anyone out of the ordinary, they turned to Kathleen and shook their heads. "Nothin' here, Kats," they said, calling her by the name they knew she hated most. "Maybe you been seein' things."

"I know what I saw," she insisted as she showed them to the door and thanked the boys for coming home with her. She started to go back in the house, then stopped: she'd wait for her sisters to come home before she went inside.

"What are you doing sitting out here?" they said when they came up the walk.

"Just enjoying the evening," she said. Kathleen wanted to talk to her mother first; no sense alarming anyone else unnecessarily.

That evening, after dinner, Kathleen asked to speak to her mother alone. "Is something wrong?" Mrs. McGuire asked, confused by Kathleen's uncharacteristic need for secrecy.

"I just want to ask you," Kathleen began, still not sure how to proceed, "if maybe you had somebody here earlier, maybe a cleaning lady or somebody. Somebody who would have been here with her little boy."

Mrs. McGuire's heart began to pound, and her face paled.

"Ma? Is it something I shouldn't know? I wasn't prying, I just came home from school and—"

"Tell me what you saw," Mrs. McGuire said, and listened carefully while Kathleen recounted her walk from school, ending when the Reid boys left the house. When she'd finished, Kathleen watched, more confused than before, as her mother shook her head. "I knew it would happen someday, but knowing it would happen didn't stop me from hoping it wouldn't." She paused a mo-

THAT'S INCREDIBLE!

ment. "Come downstairs, Kathleen. Eileen and Patricia should hear this, too."

A family meeting was convened in the sitting room, all five McGuires together. Mrs. McGuire spoke first. "Patricia," she said, "when you were just a baby, when we hadn't lived in this house very long, we had something happen here."

All three girls looked at each other, more curious than anything.

"Your Dad had been playing with you, and next thing I knew both of you were asleep on our bed. I was a little weary myself, but I didn't want to disturb such a nice picture, so I came back downstairs and stretched out on the sofa for a nap.

"I must have dozed for a minute or two, but then I heard a child crying. A child too young to be Eileen or Kathleen, not that either of them was home at the time, and too old to be Patricia. I looked up, toward the windows, and I saw a little boy standing by the door, a little boy in old-fashioned clothes. A straw hat, a sailor suit, the kind of clothes your grandfather wore. Little mite, couldn't have been more than three years old—"

THAT'S INCREDIBLE!

"Ma," Kathleen interrupted, "the boy I saw—"
Patricia and Eileen gasped.

"I know. It must have been the same boy, but let me finish. I couldn't believe my eyes at first, so I blinked hard and looked again. I could see right through that boy. I nearly killed myself getting out of that room; gave myself quite a bruise when I banged my leg on the coffee table.

"So I woke your father. He calmed me down a bit, and then we checked the room together. The boy was gone. We didn't find a thing. Not a trace."

"But if he was three when Patricia was a baby, Ma, he'd be thirteen by now. The face I saw in the window today, it was a child. It was the child you're talking about."

Mrs. McGuire had Kathleen recount, again, the events of the afternoon.

"So that's why you were sitting on the stoop when we came home!" cried Eileen. "You were scared to go inside."

"It's nothing to be ashamed of," said Mrs. McGuire. "I was scared myself."

"Now, I've never seen this boy," said Tom McGuire. "And I don't want you girls thinking I have. Once, when I was taking a nap on that same sofa, somebody yanked the blanket off and I never knew who, but that's all."

"Who is this boy, Daddy?" asked Patricia, now confused and maybe a little scared herself.

"Hush a minute, and I'll try to explain something to you," he said quietly. "Now, you remember how this place was, Eileen and Kathleen, when we first moved in. Patricia, you were too little then to remember now, but the yard was all overgrown with weeds, you almost couldn't walk out there, and the garage was hip-deep in junk and old rubbish, tires and the like."

"He wouldn't let us play in there for a long time," Kathleen explained.

"That's right. I wanted to clean it out first," Mr. McGuire said. "And I'd just begun to work on it when this thing happened to your Ma. One day, not long after she first saw that boy, I was working out in the garage and I found an old black trunk, full of photographs.

"Sorting through them, I found a whole handful of pictures of a little blond-haired boy—beautiful long, curly hair he had—in a sailor suit, posed in different places, all of them around this house."

"He showed them to me," said Mrs. McGuire, "and there was no mistaking. He was the little boy I saw standing by the door." Kathleen's mother handed her a small stack of photographs, more like heavy cards that the prints we see today. Kathleen looked at them, amazed, and her mother asked, "Is this the boy you saw?"

Kathleen looked up. "Yes ma'am, it is. But who is it?"

"We don't know who it is," Mr. McGuire said. "And I don't want this to upset you girls, but I can't not tell you. You know the shrubs by the side of the house?"

His daughters nodded.

"Behind them there's a little grave marker. The rain's worn most of the inscription off it, but you can still see where it says 'Age three years, two days.' Your Ma and I have to figure that stone marks this boy's grave."

"Then what I saw was his ghost!" Kathleen cried, raising her hands to her face.

THAT'S INCREDIBLE!

"If you really saw it, I guess that's what you saw." Mr. McGuire said, nodding.

"Daddy," asked Patricia, "will he hurt us?"

Tom McGuire reached out to stroke his daughter's hair reassuringly. "No, honey. In ten years, he's never done harm. We see him now and again, and there are times when he makes noise in the night, but he's never done harm."

"Every now and then, I've heard him beating on a little drum," Mrs. McGuire added. "And sometimes I hear him running in the hall when you're all fast asleep."

The McGuire girls, all three of them, accepted their parents' explanation of what Kathleen had seen on her way home from school. And as the weeks passed, they found they had more tales to tell.

One night, Mr. and Mrs. McGuire thought they heard walking upstairs. At first they disregarded it, thinking it was just the children. But then, listening closer, they realized that whoever was doing the walking was doing it in high-heeled shoes.

Hoping to trap the culprit, Tom went up the back stairs while Marie went up the front stairs. There was nothing upstairs but still air, and three girls asleep in their beds.

Patricia soon saw the crying boy, and one day Kathleen reported having seen a woman, dressed in old-fashioned clothes, hovering by the cold cellar. Mrs. McGuire has seen a woman peering in the kitchen window, too, but the most frequent mani-

THAT'S INCREDIBLE!

festation the family reports is the crying, and the sounds of restless feet walking upstairs.

The McGuires had a pet dog, but eventually they had to give him to friends. Why? "Twice he jumped through windows, for no reason," Mrs. McGuire told one newspaper reporter who got wind of the haunted house in Lowell. "Once he went through a screen door. I've been told dogs hear things we don't."

And the McGuires have already heard as much as they want to hear. Convinced their ghostly little housemate doesn't know he's dead, they've often spoken to him, urging him to go on up to Heaven or "wherever," and leave the house to its living occupants.

But whoever he is, the boy seems content to go on beating his tin drum in the halls on the house on Lowell's Beacon Street, to go on crying when he's lonely. Ghostly ladies come and go, possibly nursemaids of the afterworld.

"A priest came by," says Marie McGuire, "and he blessed our house. There's nothing to fear now."

She and her family will not be driven from their house. But would you spend a night in the McGuires' haunted house?

9 BEES! BEES! BEES!

It's the family picnic. You've looked forward to it all week. Unpacking the baskets you've found sandwiches, pickles, potato chips, lemonade, fried chicken, deviled eggs, buckets of iced tea, not to mention five types of dessert—including twelve-layer banana cake. You can eat yourself into a stupor, and so can everyone else. You're ignoring the ants that appear out of nowhere, doing their little insect dance wherever you'd rather they wouldn't.

But then you hear that buzz. Low, insistent, demanding to be heard. You look around, seeing a tiny form swoop by. "A bee!" you yell, and everybody—including you—jumps up and runs away.

Normal scene? Sure, pretty much everybody responds to the presence of a bee in just that manner: alarm, then rapid flight. Why? Probably because we've all been stung by bees, and therefore we all know beestings hurt.

But not everybody is afraid of bees. Take Robin Bronson, for instance. She's a student of entomology—that's the study of insects, of which the bee is one—at the University of California. Not only does Robin not run in the other direction when she detects the presence of a bee, she once stood still for letting not one, not two, but literally *thousands* of them use her for a parking place, and escaped without a single sting!

Sound incredible? Of course, but it happened.

THAT'S INCREDIBLE!

This amazing event was engineered by Dr. Norman Gary, entomologist and aviculturist (that's someone with knowledge of the care and rearing of birds)—who happens also to be one of Robin Bronson's professors at the university.

The bees who spend their lives moving from flower to flower, pollinating as they go and returning to the hive to make honey, are all females, and Dr. Gary put one of their most common shared characteristics to work in performing this amazing stunt.

Honeybees are drawn to a substance called pheromone, which duplicates the odor of the all-powerful queen bee. Robin allowed herself to be covered with pheromone, and Dr. Gary's plan went into motion.

Covered with pheromone, Robin Bronson was brought to an area near a beehive in a bright, green meadow.

Protecting himself with smoke—which bees avoid—Dr. Gary took a screen of bees and waited while Robin prepared herself. She took position, perfectly still, arms held slightly away from her sides but still very straight and still.

Then, positive that Robin was prepared and that all was in readiness, Dr. Gary released the bees. Hundreds of them. Thousands of them. And they all flew straight to Robin, landed happily somewhere on her body—and began to roam around.

"They'll come to her just as if she were a giant queen bee," Dr. Gary said as the bees piled thicker and thicker on Robin's body, creating a deep covering that ran from her waist to the top of her head.

Was Robin scared? Did Robin flinch? Not at all. She was smiling as if this solid, potentially dangerous mass of crawling insects were a million miles away.

As bees crawled across Robin's face, in fact, Dr. Gary grew concerned for the first time—after all, they might tickle her, and if they did that, Robin might begin to jiggle around. And that would frighten Robin's thousands of tiny passengers.

"There's one on your nose," Dr. Gary told her. "I think I'll brush it off." Nudging the bee with a finger, he moved it to the side of Robin's face. "You may want to just close your eyes and keep them closed," the professor advised his pupil.

Robin closed her eyes, but it wasn't easy to keep them closed. Still smiling, not a bit worried by the number of times she could be stung if the throng of bees decided to sting her, she wanted to watch what was going on! Her eyes fluttered a little, as she took quick peeks at the action.

THAT'S INCREDIBLE!

Soon, all but the surface of Robin's face was covered with crawling, happily buzzing bees.

Then Robin's nose began to wrinkle.

"Are they tickling again?" asked Dr. Gary.

"No," said Robin, "but they *are* getting a little heavy."

This came as no real surprise to Dr. Gary. "On you left arm alone there are probably five or six pounds of bees," he explained. "No wonder they're heavy. We'd better take them off soon, before you get too tired."

Take them off? How? Is there such a thing as a bee-remover? Not very likely. And what could possible be more attractive to bees than pheromone—a mass of honeysuckle?

Actually, if you ever find yourself standing around with pounds and pounds of bees wandering around on you, you'd be wise to know how

103

to remove bees. Here's how it's done.

"You're going to jump," Dr. Gary told Robin. "But before you jump, let me tell you how to do it.

THAT'S INCREDIBLE!

There are no bees on your legs, so you can kneel a little, then jump up and come down hard. Just remember one thing: Don't let your arm come down to your body, just keep it out like you've been doing. Okay? Then jump."

Crouching just a little, Robin jumped—just

THAT'S INCREDIBLE!

once, a good hard landing—and guess what? Those bees, however many thousand there were, just fell away from her body, like dust off a mop. No muss, no fuss, and Robin wasn't stung once.

And if *that* isn't incredible, what is?

Of course, you won't ever be covered by bees as Robin was—obviously it's extremely dangerous, and Dr. Gary took every precaution in performing this stunt with Robin as his subject—but most of us do have to deal with bees from time to time. Most of us, unfortunately, do all the wrong things.

If a bee begins to buzz around you head, should you blow him away with a quick gust of breath? According to Dr. Gary, that's not the most advisable method of dealing with them.

"Over millions of years," he explains, "bees have developed an incredible sensitivity to carbon dioxide—and that's in your breath—because a lot of wild animals have attacked beehives over the centuries." Thus, when a bee senses carbon dioxide, she senses danger, and she's more likely to sting the carbon-dioxide producer because she senses a threat to her nest.

So much for the idea of blowing on them.

Always better is the practice of simply standing still until the bee decides to go away, or moving slowly and carefully away from the area where the bee is hovering until her work moves her on to another spot. Waving arms, and other jerky movements, won't help a bit.

Of course, there are times when a bee stings before her victim even knows she's doing it, or in spite of his attempts to avoid the bee. What to do in *that* unfortunate situation?

Well, Dr. Norman Gary is a man of many tricks, and from his pocket he pulls another. He holds in his hand a small tube. Inside it, scratching to get out and fluttering her tiny wings, is a worker bee.

THAT'S INCREDIBLE!

What's he going to do with this worker bee? Well, Dr. Gary wouldn't want you to think his student, Robin Bronson, is the one who takes all the risks. He's going to make this bee sting him. He's not going to *let* her, he's going to *make* her!

Are you saying, "That guy must be crazy"? If Dr. Gary were anybody else, you might be right. But Dr. Gary is an expert, and he knows just what to do.

First, he shakes the little bee out of the tube and into his hand. It's incredible, how tiny this little creature is, and how much pain she can cause, and how much fear she creates in so many people! Then he picks her up—very gently, by the wings—and presses her stinger against the tip of his finger. Then he speaks very loudly, to startle the bee and force her to sting him—for after all, a bee stings because that is her only defense against enemies.

The bee does just as Dr. Gary wants, plunging her stinger in his—can you believe it?—willing finger. He pulls her gently away from his finger, and as he does so the stinging mechanism is torn from her body. She'll die soon; bees don't live long after they've stung, and therefore they've risked their own lives. Dr. Gary puts her back in the tube, then points to the tiny blob on the tip of his finger. It is, as a closer look shows, a small drop of poison attached to a barb.

And it's throbbing! "See what it's doing?" says Dr. Gary. "What it's doing is very much like what a doctor does when he gives an injection. As it

THAT'S INCREDIBLE!

pumps, the venom is forced through the stinger and into my hand. Just like geting an injection, only this injection isn't going to make me feel any better. But watch it pump for a second . . ."

Isn't he going to *do* something? Wipe it off, or put a stop to this venom pumping into his skin? He will, and soon he shows the best way to do it.

Using a fingernail, Dr. Gary quickly scrapes the mass away from his finger, pulling the stinger out cleanly because he has scraped with the direction of the stinger. Most of the venom has not had a chance to pump in yet, and—although Dr. Gary will still have a slight sore spot—it won't be nearly as bad as it could have been had he simply let that tiny, natural syringe of venom do its job.

He's a brave man. And what he's just done is absolutely incredible.

10 / LOST CHILD?

Nothing tears at a mother's heartstrings like the idea of a lost child, looking for its home, wandering around in ever-widening circles that take it farther from the place it wants to go.

A father who learns his child has gotten lost on the way home from school, or band practice, or a Little League baseball game will call the police, alert friends, patrol the surrounding blocks in his car, unable to rest until Janet or Timmy is home and safe again.

No one likes to think of being lost—there are few more frustrating feelings—or even of anyone *else* being lost.

But ask yourself, and then answer yourself honestly:

If a child stopped you on the street and said, "I'm lost. Will you help me?" what would you do? Stop and help him, or walk on and leave the bewildered, maybe terrified youngster alone to fend for himself?

Now be honest. Would you?

Chances are better that a small-towner would help. That's what two psychologists, Bibb Latane and John Darley, decided in 1970. They found that city folks are less likely to lend a hand in an emergency, and there's an interesting reason why. Possibly because everyone assumes someone *else* will do something, nobody does *any*thing. When a large group of people is standing around when an accident happens, chances are that no one will go for help; if there are only two people there when the same accident happens, chances are good that one of them will provide or obtain assistance.

Boiled down to simple terms, that means that city people would be more likely to pass the lost child by than small-town people, simply because there are more of them.

But is it really true? Could a busy, self-absorbed city slicker—a New Yorker, for instance—really pass a lost child without stopping to dry the child's eyes and give his mother a call?

Harold Takooshian, associate professor of psychology at New York's Fordham University, wanted to find out for himself, so he began a study of his

THAT'S INCREDIBLE!

own—prompted by Stanley Milgram at the City University of New York, and designed with his help.

"Stanley Milgram assigned us to test empirically the traditional wisdom that people in cities are more indifferent to the suffering of others," explains Takooshian. "We tried to pick a scene that was as touching as possible. We decided the ideal incident was a lost child. Children are lost every day in the city and often reach the point of tears—they get scared, they get frightened. The question we wanted answered was: what percentage of New Yorkers would stop and help a lost child in the middle of Manhattan—a child asking for any kind of sympathy or help."

And here's how he got his answer.

Children between the ages of six and ten were asked to play the role of lost boy or girl. Each stood on a busy street corner and asked approaching strangers, "I'm lost. Can you call my house?" A story had been prepared for anyone who stopped: the child explained that he and his mother had been shopping but somehow got separated. If the stranger offered help, the child showed the Good Samaritan a card bearing his family's home phone number.

Naturally, an observer stood close by to make sure the child came to no harm, and also recorded the sex, race and approximate age of anyone who stopped, along with whatever conversation passed between stranger and child. The observer also kept track of the number of people in the general area, as well as the number of people who could hear the child's request.

All bases were covered. The child's real parent, or a guardian, would appear suddenly in the event one of the strangers offered to call the child's parents or take him home. Shouting the child's name

THAT'S INCREDIBLE!

and babbling thanks, the parent would conveniently dash from his or her nearby hiding place.

The plan seemed foolproof. The rest was up to the people of New York City.

Takooshian started small, planting nine-year-old Jackie in a Brooklyn shopping center two days before Christmas. Jackie approached one Brooklynite who ignored her, a second who snapped, "So what's your problem, kid? I'm lost, too," and a third who responded as the first stranger had. Takooshian gave up and went home.

But Takooshian tried again, not only in Manhattan but in four major cities and twelve small towns, using fourteen children. His results were fascinating.

In the cities, including bustling midtown Manhattan, 46 percent of the strangers approached by a "lost child" offered some sort of assistance, compared to 72 percent in smaller towns.

But even the refusals of help in the city were interesting. Rejecting the child abruptly, some would swerve by or step around, speed up in order to pass him more quickly, some shook their heads instead of actually uttering the word "No," and occasionally they even went so far as to pull themselves out of the child's grasp. Then there were those who would hand the child money as they passed him by, mostly small change, before leaving him behind.

On one extraordinary occasion, a man in New York City—an elderly gentleman—stopped and talked to the "lost" boy, patted him on the head, finally shook his head and declined to help. But then he did an amazing thing. He actually crossed the street and waited behind a lamppost, and from this nearby observation spot kept an eye on the safety of a child he had, only minutes ago, refused to actively help. For fifteen minutes he stood, silently craning his neck and watching others refuse their aid, as he had. Finally, when a woman stopped and agreed to help the boy, the elderly man deserted his post and went about his business. Incredible!

Those who actually offered help sometimes did so in strange ways. Some gave the child a dime and suggested he make the call himself. One said to the child, "Go into that restaurant. Your mother's waiting for you there." She wasn't, of course, but the stranger had rid himself of the child without really involving himself in the problem!

Some who stopped to help did it in interesting ways, too. One New Yorker immediately asked the lost girl if she'd had lunch, and would she like to get something to eat before being taxied home. Another, not sure what to do, asked a second stranger for advice. That stranger stopped a third, and so it went. By the time the child's parent rushed forward to "find" him, the child had disappeared inside a nine-person squad of rescuers.

Responses may have differed, but the statistics were clear: a lost child in downtown Manhattan had a fifty-fifty chance of being helped by the first New York stranger he asked.

Psychological studies of city dwellers offer some answers as to why only one in two New Yorkers would rise to the occasion. Takooshian has his own favorite explanation for the phenomenon. The reason is that urban life demands so much from those who live it, that they just naturally make life easier on themselves by being less involved with other people. There's so much noise, so much going on for the city dweller, that he eventually learns to ignore the constant demands on him. For that reason, he stops saying "Hello" to everyone he meets (sure, that habitual "good morning" given to all in Smalltown, USA, is second nature, but there are 8 million people in New York City!), he's not likely to do favors for people he doesn't know, and—five times out of ten—he even ignores a child who says, "I'm lost. Will you help me?"

Now that may sound heartless, but to people who live in cities, it's a way of life that helps keep them sane.

But what does this new knowledge tell you? Well, two pieces of advice spring instantly to mind:

1. If you're a child, be sure you only get lost in small towns.

2. If you're a citified adult and a small child—or anyone else—asks for help, don't count on someone else to do it. Open up just a little, and give that little guy a break.

You'll feel better for it, and so will he!

119

11 INSIDE TINY TEARS

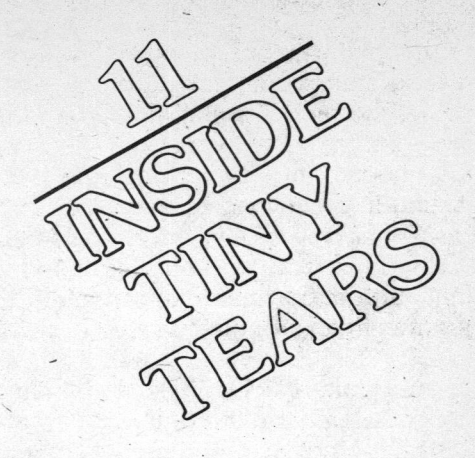

Are tears something you take for granted, something you don't think too much about? If so, then you ought to pay a little more attention, because tears are more helpful than you think.

Ever wonder why people blink so often? Every blink gives your eyelids their nature-given opportunity to wash the surface of your eyes with—guess what?—tears, and keep your corneas moist.

If you're chopping onions, or working with some other irritating stuff, your tear ducts will step in again and set the tears flowing, this time to help soothe the irritation.

But what about the times when you're in a movie theater, taking in a showing of, say, *Love Story*, and just as Oliver crawls onto the hospital bed to hold his dying Jennifer close, your eyes flood with tears? What purpose do those tears serve? Are they soothing some irritant or keeping your corneas moist?

Neither one, really. But Dr. William H. Frey II, a biochemist in the Department of Psychiatry at St. Paul—Ramsey Medical Center in Minnesota, thinks such tears—those shed by people under emotional pressure—serve a unique, and extremely important, purpose all their own. Research he's doing right now is intended to prove just that.

At the medical center, Dr. Frey and his team of researchers are conducting pioneering experiments on the nature of tears and crying. For the first time, sensitive instruments are being used to analyze the subtle chemistry of tears.

Frey hopes the research will confirm his belief that emotional tears help remove harmful substances from the body. Biochemists already believe that people who are sad or depressed are suffering from chemical imbalances—so it would be one of Mother Nature's neater tricks if crying was a way of cleaning bad chemicals out of the body and getting things back to a happy norm. No wonder we feel better after a good cry!

Unfortunately, studying tears isn't the easiest thing in the world to do, as Dr. Frey has discovered.

"It is difficult to collect tears from people, espe-

THAT'S INCREDIBLE!

123

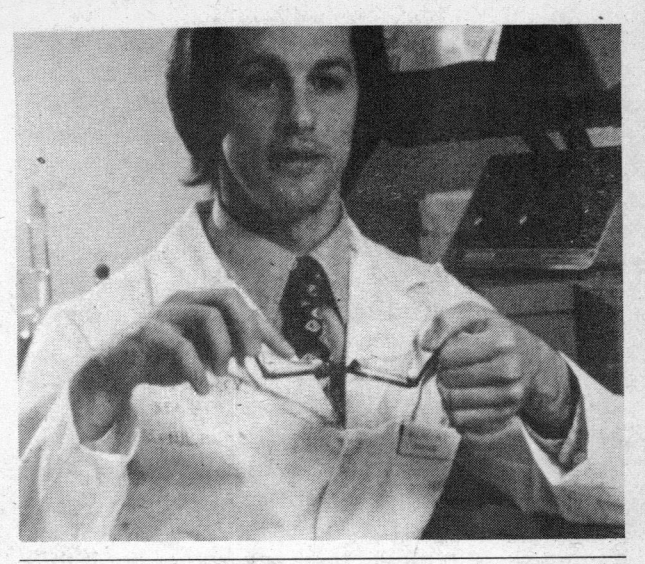

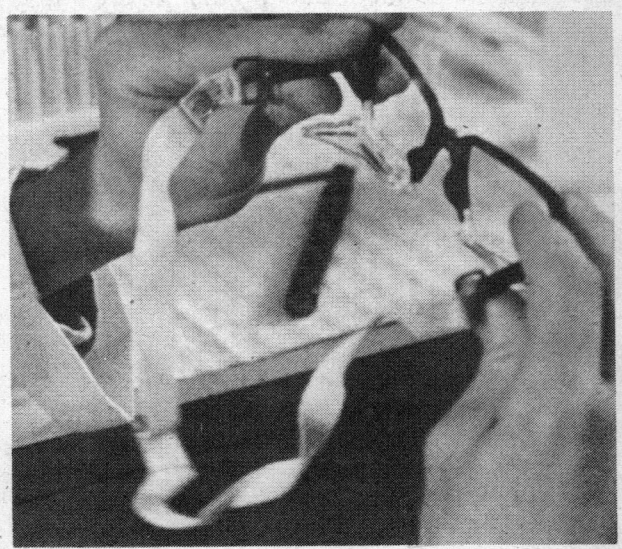

cially emotional tears," he admits. "Even the irritant-induced tears that we collect in response to onion vapor have been something of problem."

He usually does it like this: To obtain irritant-induced tears, he uses—of course—onions, and finds U.S. Number One onions are the most effective at getting people to cry. After exposing the eyes to onion vapor for a short time, almost any subject will begin to cry. Dr. Frey then catches the tears by holding a flat-sided test tube under the subject's watery eyes.

Collecting emotional tears, however, presents massive problems that Dr. Frey hasn't yet altogether conquered.

"To begin with," he explains, "people who might cry easily over a movie if they saw it in a private studio or at home or in the darkness and anonymity of a movie theater may not cry if they see the same movie in a medical center study where they realize they are being observed and where they have the feeling that they are expected to cry regardless of what you tell them ahead of time."

One answer to this has been to let the subjects collect their own tears, by giving each one a flat-sided tear-collector and a box-seat for a guaranteed tearjerker like the James Caan weeper *Brian's Song*.

Dr. Frey will take whatever he can get—after all, no tears, no research—but he certainly has his "druthers":

"Ideally," he admits, "we would've liked to be able to collect our emotional tears from our subjects who are watching the sad movie by having the investigator sitting there and simply collecting tears as they come out of the eyes, but obviously this

THAT'S INCREDIBLE!

125

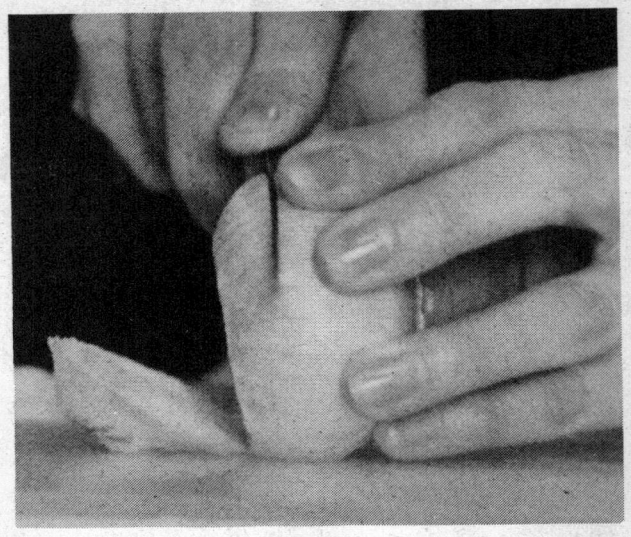

would've interfered very seriously with the emotional response to the movie.

"Consequently, we tried to come up with a method that would cause the least interference." Dr. Frey holds up a pair of strap-on glasses, a new-fangled tear-catching contraption that he's about to explain.

"Originally we thought we could have a pair of special glasses designed. These are the glasses that

THAT'S INCREDIBLE!

we originally tried, which would have no lenses but would instead have small glass cups below. The frames would fit so that the cups would fit against the face, and the individual would simply wear these glasses, collecting the tears without any effort at all. Then at the end of the movie we could come in and collect the tears from the glass cups."

The glasses didn't work very well, Dr. Frey continues, "because it's a fact that the architecture of people's faces differs quite a bit. We could make a pair of these glasses and the cups *would* fit right against the face on some individuals. Unfortunately, they wouldn't fit other individuals, which kept them from being universally effective."

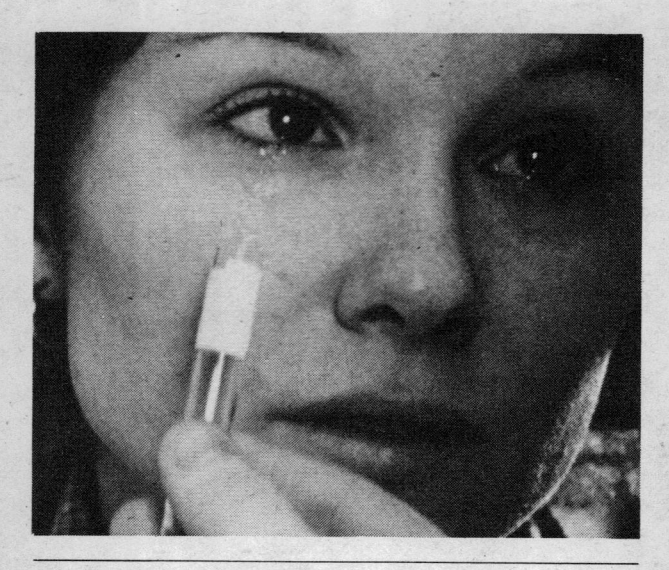

Such setbacks, however, are what makes science interesting, so Dr. Frey went back to the drawing board and is still working on devising a method of collecting tears that will not hamper the emotions of the tear-research subjects.

The research—when the team has enough tears to work with—is showing interesting results so far. Studies show, for instance, that chemicals known as *catecholamines* are released into the bloodstream when a person is under stress. Dr. Frey has been able to confirm that emotional tears contain catecholamines, which indicates he's right to be-

THAT'S INCREDIBLE!

lieve the tears we cry when we're sad *do* rid our bodies of chemicals that may be creating our sadness.

So. What does all this mean?

Well, if Dr. Frey is correct in his theories, it means you're far better off to cry than to choke back your tears. As a matter of fact, Dr. Frey's research may even give new meaning to the phrase "crying it out," and may demonstrate what wonders a good cry can work.

Research may even prove that not crying may be hazardous to your health. Non-criers could be more prone to ulcers, emotional disorders, and maybe even a complete loss of touch with their feelings.

Which is good news for those of you who go through boxes of tissues each time you go to a sad movie. If you get embarrassed when those eye-faucets open up, don't be anymore: you know what's good for you, so cry away!

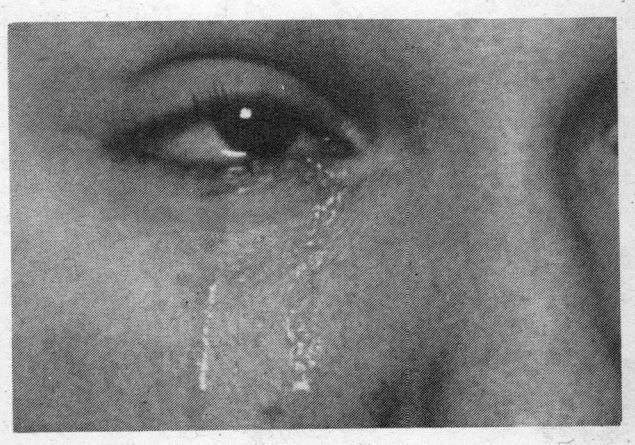

12
DAVID'S DREAM

If you had been standing in David Booth's bedroom on the early morning of May 16, 1979, you'd have seen with your eyes something frightening—but not nearly as frightening as what David was seeing inside his head.

David Booth was sound asleep, dreaming, tossing from side to side. If you'd been watching him, you might have said he was a restless sleeper. Well,

131

a restless sleeper this young Cincinatti man might be, but it was not restlessness that was bothering David's sleep that night. It was the dream, the home movie going on inside the twenty-three-year-old's head. His tossing would not stop it. Nothing would stop it, until it was ready to come to an end of its own accord.

In his sleep, David was looking over a vast, empty field. In one direction lay a downed tree, lying at a diagonal, as if some spoiled giant-child had pulled it up by its roots and then, bored of the game, had thrown it back to earth again.

Above him flew an airplane. Not just an airplane, but a jet—a monstrously big one. Metallic gray, it glinted in the bright sunlight, and as David looked at it he poised his hand over his eyes as a shield. He squinted, and saw red and blue markings on the fuselage and tail. It was an American Airlines jet, taking off. Briefly, David wondered where it was going.

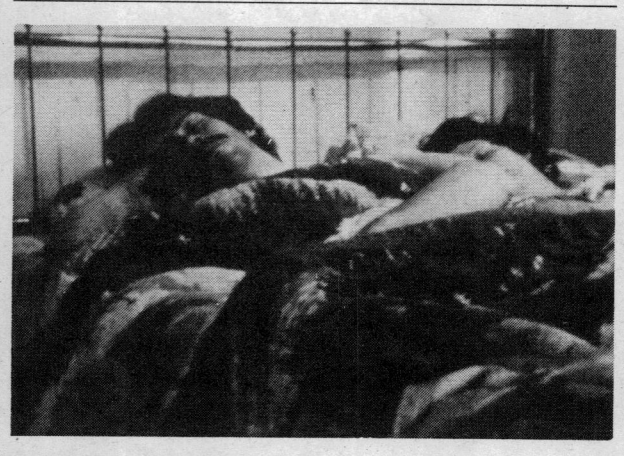

THAT'S INCREDIBLE!

The jet's rumblings distracted David from his thoughts. The sound seemed jerky, not quite right, and it occurred to David that all was not well with the jet. There was no feeling of impending doom, no notion that the gigantic machine might crash; the sound of the engine simply seemed to him odd.

Then a strange thing happened: the plane turned on its side, dipped its wing as if to salute David, still watching below. The plane, in that position—its wings pointing north and south, its nose and tail indicating west and east—seemed to be making the sign of the cross.

Was the plane asking for some kind of blessing? What for? What was it about to do?

And then David knew. As quickly as it had dipped its wing, the massive airliner turned on its back and dove straight down, crashing straight into the ground.

David watched in horror as what had been a sleek gray airborne monument to man's triumph over nature became a pile of wreckage from which spewed billowing clouds of orange and gray and red fire. There was a sound—was it real, or did the David in David's dream only imagine he heard it?—like hundreds of souls suddenly crying out in pain.

The David in David's dream watched, struck where he stood by terror such as none he'd ever known. And when the sound had died out, he turned to run, and...

... woke up.

David stared at the ceiling above him for a second or two, reassuring himself that he was home in bed, freezing forever in his mind the truth of the

THAT'S INCREDIBLE!

matter: that there was no blue sky above him, but rather a pale white ceiling from which no plane would ever plummet toward tragedy.

Awake now, relocated but not reassured, David threw the covers back, sat up, and put both feet on the floor. The fire was still bright in his eyes, and he rubbed them until the flames went away. Then he looked at the clock. It was too early to start getting ready for work, but there was no way he was going to roll over and go back to sleep. In his sleep he might wander back to that field.

David Booth had already seen as much of that wind-swept field as he ever in his life wanted to see.

He stood up, stretched a little and shivered at the memory of the dream, and stumbled into the kitchen to make coffee. It was behind him.

David went to his job, as a car-rental manager in Cincinatti. The dream faded into the back of his mind and he worked over his desk, computing mileage, seeing to the details of his business. At day's end he went home, had dinner, passed the evening, and went to bed.

Snuggling down into the covers, assuming his favorite sleeping position, David dozed, sank into

THAT'S INCREDIBLE!

ever-deeper levels of sleep, and finally arrived at the point at which the brain, refusing to rest completely, begins work its night shift—the point at which sleepers begin to dream.

And as the movie screen in David's mind flickered with light and became a recognizable scene, the waking sense of David's mind drew back and said, "No, please, not again."

For in David's dream, the dream David was standing, looking out over a vast field, seeing to one side a downed tree, while overhead . . .

David's waking sense was powerless, as it had been the night before. The dream would finish whenever it liked, not before, and as the dream David watched in horror, the big jet dipped its wing, turned on its back, and crashed into fiery wreckage.

And then David Booth woke up, reoriented himself, and sat up, terrified even more than he had been the previous morning. Never in his life had he had the identical dream two nights in a row. Was he about to die? Had he seen a movie about plane crashes that frightened him more than he thought?

David rose, made coffee as he had the morning before, went to work, and tried to put the dream into the back of his mind, where it had slipped naturally only twenty-four hours earlier. Today it would not be banished so easily. It nagged him, and occasionally he would find himself lapsing into thought instead of working, chewing on his pencil, trying to figure out the dream.

That night, getting ready for bed, David found he was putting off the inevitable. Just as he was about to get into bed, he would think of one more shirt that needed putting in the hamper, one more lock

THAT'S INCREDIBLE!

that needed checking. David was dreading sleep.

And with good reason. That, night, the American Airlines jet crashed in David's dream for the third straight night.

In the morning, he went to work. Over and over he would find himself being seized by waves and waves of pure sorrow. Was it the souls of the crash screaming again, reaching David even at his desk in broad daylight? His work was slipping.

Recurrence of the dream on the fourth, fifth, and sixth nights didn't help his mental state. On the morning of the seventh dream David went to work, tried to steep himself in what he was paid to do, but eventually pushed it all to one side and grabbed the telephone directory. He dialed the number given for the Cincinatti office of the Federal Aeronautics Administration, and reached Paul Williams there.

Trying to be calm, trying not to sound as crazy as he knew he must sound, David explained to Williams what had been happening to him each night and related every detail of the dream. He had no trouble remembering, and winced as he recalled for Williams the crash itself.

"I'm not sure I know why I'm calling you," David said. "But it's been seven nights in a row, the same dream, the same American Airlines jet. I don't know whether it means anything, Mr. Williams, and I'm not some crackpot who's going to try to get you to ground every American plane in the world."

"I understand, Mr. Booth," said Williams, who had the gut reaction that this man truly was no crackpot. "It's quite a vivid dream. Seven nights of that would unnerve anybody."

Williams offered to call the FAA regional office in Atlanta, and to make a general advisement to the airline. "It's really the only thing I can do," he said.

"I appreciate it," David said, feeling that however little good it would do, at least he'd gotten this off his chest. Maybe a little action would shake the dream.

David Booth turned back to his work and tried unsuccessfully to immerse himself. That night he went home and had the dream for the eighth time.

The following night brought the dream's ninth appearance.

On the early morning of Friday, May 25, David lay in a fitful sleep, resigned to the idea of having the dream again and yet still hoping it would go away. As he had expected, the dream invaded his rest, and at its conclusion he sat up quickly, looked around feverishly to insure for the tenth time that he was home in bed and all was well.

On this tenth morning of the dream, however, there was a difference. Somehow he knew that he had suffered the dream for the last time, that he was free of it now forever. It was gone.

THAT'S INCREDIBLE!

But this inner knowledge did nothing for his state of mind. He drove to work and arrived only to have forgotten entirely that he'd made the drive. The trip had flown out of his mind. He sat down at his desk and decided to call Paul Williams one more time, thinking it might ease his mind. But David Booth was as upset at this moment as he could ever remember having been in his entire life. His whole thought process was disrupted; he couldn't concentrate on anything.

Sorrow had seized control of him, body and soul. Constantly on the verge of tears, he was totally unable to function.

Miles away, at the Cincinatti office of the FAA, Paul Williams's fingers itched. He felt compelled to call the Atlanta office, tell them for the second time about David Booth and his recurring dream. It baffled Williams: he felt drawn to the telephone as if to a magnet.

Finally he gave in to his impulses and picked up the receiver.

He got Jack Barker on the line.

"It's been ten dreams in a row," he told Barker. "I had to call and tell you."

Barker listened, as baffled as to how to proceed as Williams and Booth had been. "Look," he said, "can't he remember *any*thing else? If he could nail down anything else, when it took place or where, just one number off the plane."

"He's not predicting anything," Williams explained. "He's not that kind of guy. He's just a kid who's had this freaky dream ten times in a row, Jack. It gets to him, which is understandable. What's maybe not so understandable is that it gets to me, too."

141

"Well," sighed Barker, "as long as the airline knows, what else can we do?"

"Nothing, I suppose," Williams admitted resignedly. "I just had to call and tell you this morning made an even ten."

There wasn't much else to say, and nothing else to be done. Barker and Williams hung up.

Back at the car-rental office, David Booth was ready to hang it up. Being at work wasn't doing him or anyone else any good.

David Booth left work early on May 25. As he got in his car, the clocks in Cincinatti gave the time as 4:00 P.M.

In Chicago, at that city's sprawling O'Hare Airport, the time was 3:00 P.M. Air traffic was heavy; this was Friday afternoon and the beginning of Memorial Day weekend, one of the busiest travel weekends of the year. Summer was just beginning, all over the country.

On one of the airport's many runways, a massive jet, a DC-10, was waiting for takeoff instructions. Its engines roared as it sat, motionless. Its fuselage glinted in the sunlight, a shiny metallic surface producing the glare. Along the plane's sides were red-and-blue-lettered words and symbols: American Airlines, and its symbol, a bird in flight.

On the radio, a voice crackled. American Airlines Flight 191 was ready and cleared for takeoff.

She taxied down the runway, and when the time was right her nose came off the ground, her tail followed, and Flight 191 was in flight.

Anyone on the ground, gazing up, will never forget what came next.

Just as she was leaving the airport, the big American Airlines jet did something strange: still

THAT'S INCREDIBLE!

flying at low altitude, she turned one wing up, thereby dipping the other. And in an instant, she dove into a hideous, fiery crash.

American Flight 191, a silvery DC-10, had ended in tragedy. It was the worst airline disaster in American history; 272 people died.

It had happened, almost to the last detail, just as David Booth had described it in his recurring dream.

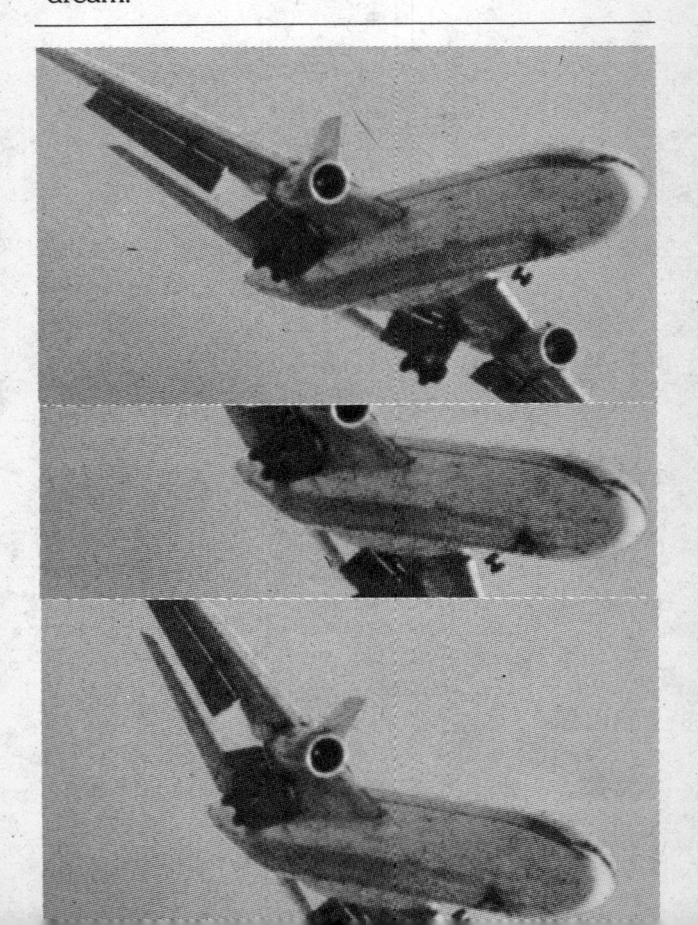

THAT'S INCREDIBLE!

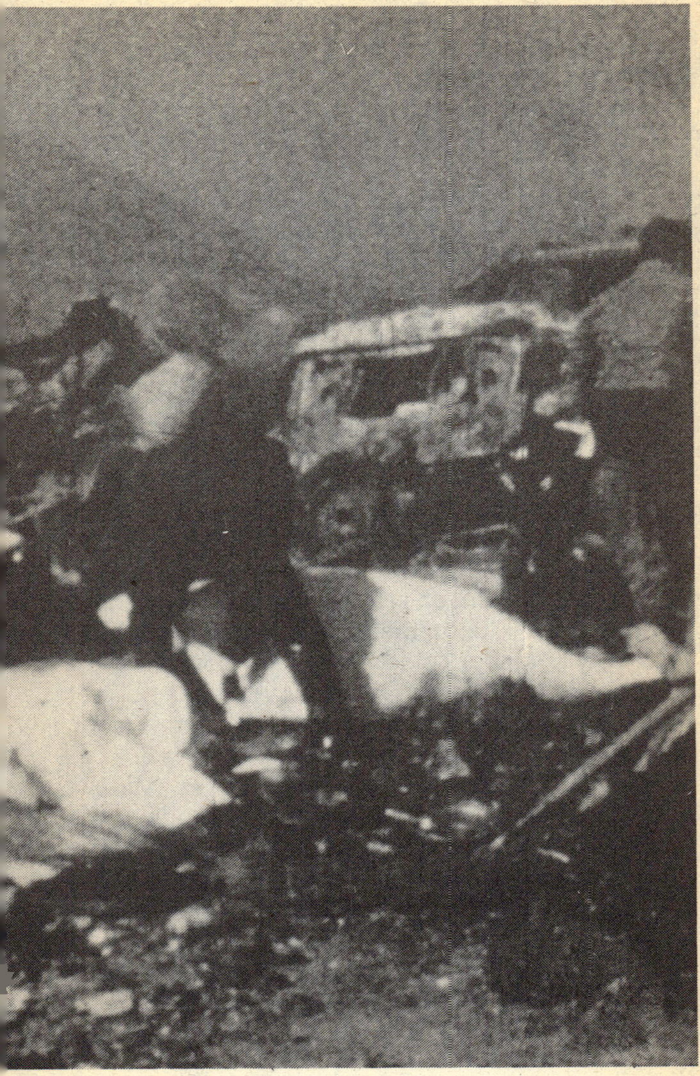

David learned of the crash at home. When he saw a photographer's extraordinary photograph of Flight 191 with one wing dipped, he thought it was like seeing a movie still from his dream.

Distraught and in tears, David Booth called Paul Williams.

"If there had been something, just anything we could have done," David said over and over.

But what could have been done had been done. Tragically, it had not been enough, but at least they'd tried, Williams assured him. David fell apart emotionally while talking with Williams, who brought him back to earth a little and convinced him not to blame himself for what had happened.

As the FAA's Jack Barker later said: "It was just uncanny, how close Mr. Booth was in seeing in his dream what actually happened. He saw things that did not occur, he saw irregularities that weren't there, but he saw an awful lot of similarities."

And he has an answer to the problem that plagued David Booth, that of helplessness. Wasn't there anything that could have been done?

"There's no FAA policy or government policy that I'm aware of for handling dreams or premonitions.

"I guess I could ask you the question: 'What would you think of my spending public funds, taxpayers' funds, to chase down somebody's dream or premonition?'"

To hear David Booth tell his story is to believe he might well have used his own money to chase the dream down, had he known how. But he has learned to live with what happened during those ten incredible nights, and any guilt he felt is gone now.

THAT'S INCREDIBLE!

"Maybe we fell short," he says, "but there was nothing we could blame ourselves for. We didn't have that much to go on, but at least we tried. At least we can rest assured that we did try to do something.

"We made an attempt, and we failed. Still, I can't help but think that—if there had just been somebody we could have talked to—it could have been prevented."

For ten consecutive nights in May, 1979, David Booth had a dream that appears to have foretold the future.

What could anyone do with such a dream?
What would *you* do?

13 GHOSTLY ADOPTION SERVICE

In Sonoma, California, a pale young woman with long, blond, gossamer hair sits quietly on the floor in her living room. Candlelight flickers around her. At first there is no sound, but as moments pass a whispering sound begins to move in the air. Listen closely: the young woman is reading from a paper she holds in her lap. She holds her arms open, as if to embrace the room, and then her fingers beckon.

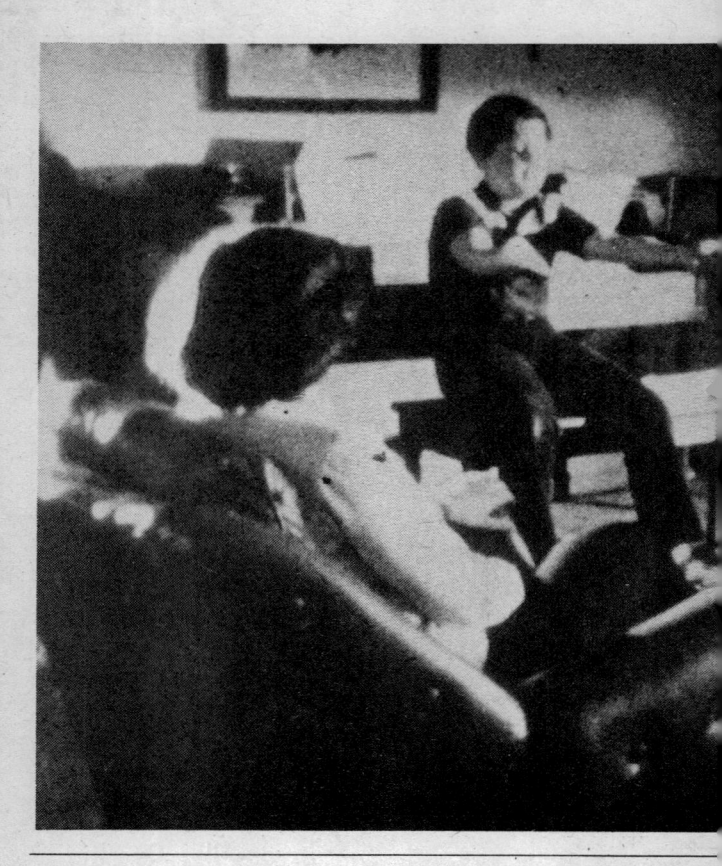

"Who will honor this request?" she murmurs.

Days later, in San Rafael, California, a chubby ten-year-old boy sits in his darkened living room. His eyes are closed. Around him sit his family—mother, father, sister—their eyes also closed. The room is stuffy because the windows and doors are closed tight. The boy is concentrating; his eyes are pressed closed. Suddenly, as if he has finally under-

THAT'S INCREDIBLE!

stood something deep down inside, the boy extends his arms straight in front of him. He speaks: "John Sebastian, welcome to this house." But no one besides the boy and his family is there.

What's going on with these people?

The woman is Sande Marsolan, a thirty-two-year-old ex-nurse who runs the world's most unique adoption agency. The boy is Sean

151

McEowen, who's adopted one of Sande's orphans. Sande is the owner and sole proprietress of the Ghost Adoption Agency, and John Sebastian is Sean's newly-adopted ghost.

If the whole idea of adopting a ghost sounds crackpot to you, get ready to change your mind. Sande's many satisfied customers will be only too happy to change it for you.

Sande herself was the first satisfied customer, and she herself didn't even know she was in the market for an orphan ghost.

"When I was twenty years old," she says, "I realized that I had a ghost around me. His name is Jeffrey, and for the past twelve years I have had such an enriched life knowing this ghost that I wanted to share what I had found. So I started a ghost adoption agency."

For a fee of $185 (it started at $20 and has risen to the $185 high, although some pay less) Sande will summon a personal ghost for adoption. The ghost's sex, personality, and other characteristics can usually be tailored to the desire of the client.

What Sande does is act as a conduit between the ghost—or, as she says, the "entity"—and the client. First, she receives a letter from the client, asking about the agency and how to go about adopting a ghost. She sends the client a form to fill out, and when she gets back the completed form, Sande begins to look for the right entity for the client to adopt.

Sitting quietly, she concentrates, stretches out her hands, and asks, "Who will honor this request?"

A ghost will then make him- or herself known to Sande.

THAT'S INCREDIBLE!

Sande believes the people who contact her, wanting to adopt a ghost, already have an entity surrounding them. Sande feels her basic purpose in the relationship is to make the formal introduction.

Once the entity has appeared to Sande, his detailed synopsis is written up by Sande and she sends it along to the client. Interestingly, she finds some clients have confrontations with their ghostly adoptees before they receive Sande's letter in the mail, while some clients can wait weeks for their first meeting with the entity. Sande herself says the standard way of doing things involves the ghost lingering at her home in Sonoma before moving into his newly adopted home.

Sande has yet to disappoint a client, and she's now running the agency full time. She keeps in touch with all her old clients and their entities, always ready to help out if any problems arise. Few do, however.

Word of Sande Marsolan's very unusual service has spread—helped just a little by coverage in newspapers, magazines and television—but Sande is determined to limit the number of clients she will accept. At present, twelve per month is her limit.

Gentle-natured, warm with a natural sweetness, Sande devotes herself to this small number of clients because she genuinely cares about the people and entities with whom she deals, wants them to be happy with each other, and always asks her clients for a confirmation letter—just so she'll know they're happy with the ghost they've adopted.

One could ask, of course, how a person gets into the business of sending out ghosts for adoption. There is, of course, Sande's experience with her own entity, Jeffrey, and her desire for others to have a relationship like theirs. Also, there's Sande's real belief that most people have an entity who is never far away, an entity they unfortunately never come to know. Sande thinks that's sad for both parties.

"An entity needs three things," she says. "He needs to be loved, he needs to be needed, and he needs to be acknowledged." So do people still living on the earth, so a relationship between a living soul and an entity seems like a marriage made in heaven.

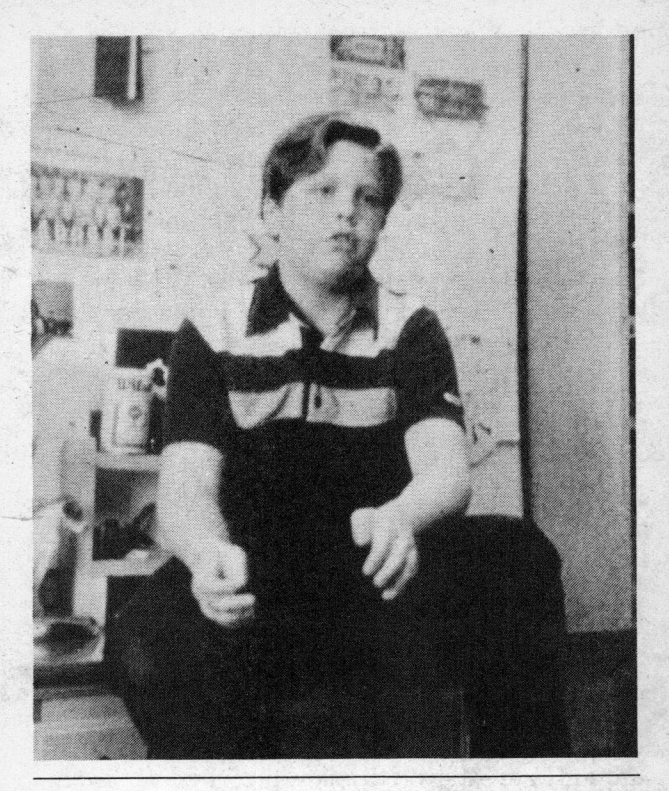

"A common misnomer is the people who have haunted houses," Sande says. "They say, 'Yes, I've got a ghost,' but they don't try to relate. The children who have adopted ghosts tell me that they are doing better in school. Your conscious awareness definitely increases by getting in contact with the spiritual realm."

One child who adopted a ghost was young Sean

McEowen. He doesn't mention being a sudden straight-A student, but he does talk with real enthusiasm about the newest member of his family. He also sheds more light on the whole adoption process.

"In order to bring the ghost into the house we had to have a ceremony," he explains. He had asked Sande for a teenager from the Colonial era who was believed to have participated in the American Revolution. When she wrote back, informing Sean that an entity had come forward to honor his request, she also told him how to establish contact with his new ghost.

"My family and I all went out into the living room, closed all the windows and doors so the room would be perfectly quiet, then sat down in chairs. I told them, 'Think about just one thing: John Sebastian.' And when they were all doing that I said, 'John Sebastian, we welcome you to our house.'"

The rest is the McEowen family history.

"After we adopted the ghost," Sean continues, "strange things started to happen. Like, these two big ravens—and we don't even *have* ravens around here—began to follow me wherever I went. And whenever I was thinking about John Sebastian, then I'd look at a building or something, one of the ravens would fly up and just sit there until I'd blocked the thought out of my mind."

Sean thinks a moment, then recalls something even newer. "Last night the alarm in the hall turned on without reason." Other incidents—starting up music boxes, knocking pictures off walls, etc.—indicate John Sebastian is quite a mischief-maker.

Sande suggested Sean talk to his ghost a lot,

THAT'S INCREDIBLE!

confide in him, which he does. The boy feels the entity's presence around him constantly. "Whenever I'm feeling bad, whenever I have a problem or something," says Sean, "I can talk to him. I can sit down and talk to him and feel that someone's listening."

That has to be a good feeling, for man or boy.

Geroge Schmidt is a thirty-year-old man who's taken advantage of Sande's agency.

"I'm sitting here," George—an up-and-coming salesman—begins, "telling you that it's real, but there are still people who say, 'No way, it *can't* be real.' That's what we were brought up to believe, that it's not real, but it is. It's really real!"

George read about Sande in a newspaper, and wrote to her asking for an active ghost with a good head for business. She matched him up with a ghost he refers to only as "Harold"; that's not the ghost's real name, but he was someone very famous in his earthly life and now he prefers to remain anonymous.

Unlike most of Sande's clients, George has actually seen his ghost—well, in a way. Harold first appeared as a black shadow, but he's also been known to manifest himself as a cluster of blinking lights. George also hears Harold bumping around, and once even heard him sneeze!

George always knows when Harold's around: the entity causes George to feel cold—although not necessarily a *bad* kind of cold. George once tried to photograph his unearthly friend, but when he had the film developed, only the attempted shots of Harold turned out completely black.

"One night I was coming out of my office upstairs after doing some paperwork. I was really tired." George grins to himself as he remembers. "I was walking into my bedroom and I remembered I had forgotten something. I spun around real quick and—*bam!*—I ran into him. But I thought, 'Nah, it couldn't be.'

"So I went back to my office and picked up what I wanted. I turned around real quick so that I hit him again and I said, 'Will you get out of my way?' At first I thought he had a friend with him. You know,

THAT'S INCREDIBLE!

the guy goes out, gets himself a date and comes back..."

Harold is a constant source of amusement for George. He's also a good companion who gives George solid help in his business work.

In short, Harold has made George's life better than it was in the pre-Harold days. George freely admits that "before I got him my life was not really the pits, but just kind of—well, some you win, some you lose." He winks with just a slightly wicked look. "Now, most of them I win!"

Don't get the idea that only men and boys adopt Sande's ghosts. Women have adopted many, and one *group* of women applied, too. Five beauticians

THAT'S INCREDIBLE!

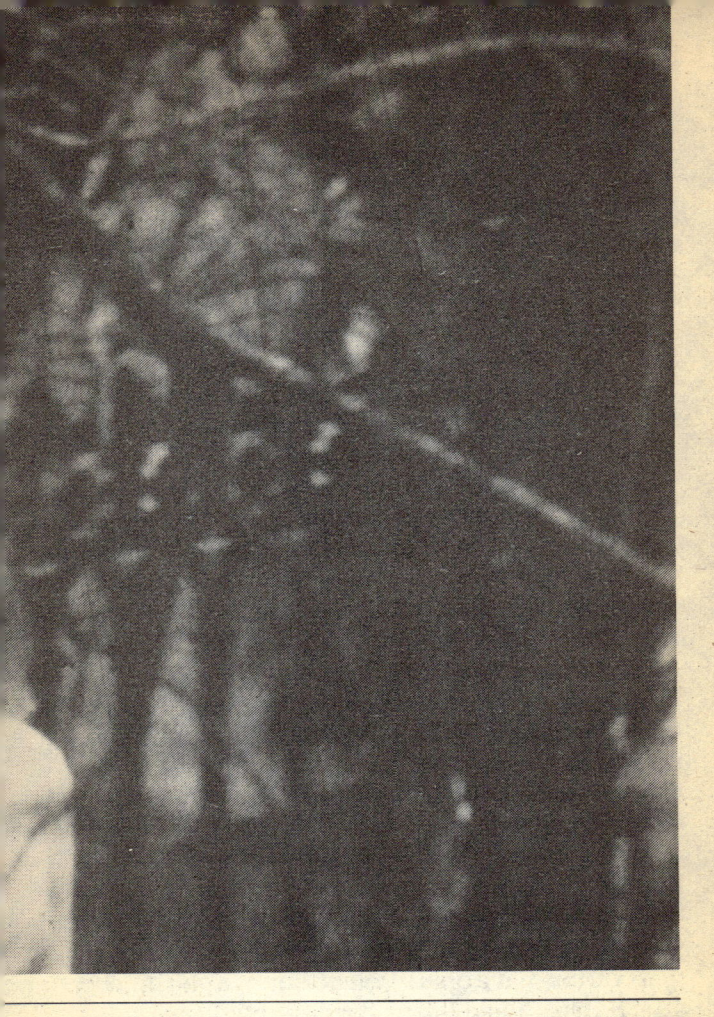

at Gazebo Hair Fashions in San Rafael, California, wrote to Sande asking for a ghost with a sense of humor, one who could "boogie." They all chipped in to pay for him, and Sande presented their case to the spirit world.

One of the beauticians tells the story:

"We thought it would be fun to adopt a ghost, so we sent in our letter and our check and subsequently, through communication with Sande, we received the Marquis de Sade as our ghost to adopt.

"Since then we've had neat little things happening, and he lets us know when he wants some attention." She indicates a small hand-mirror hung from a nail on the wall. "Maybe the little hand mirror will start swinging. If it does, we talk to him awhile, and then it's fine and he settles down."

A second beautician adds: "He doesn't really do anything harmful, just playful little pranks. He swings mirrors, and occasionally drops a coffee cup. He hides things, and he's opened a few doors, a few cabinets. Just little things like that. It's kinda nice . . ." There's an inward-looking smile on her face, and you know she's serious.

A third, giggly beautician chimes in as she works on a client's hair. "Having the marquis around now isn't quite the same thing as having him around the way he was before. He's mellowed with age, like wine." Privately, the ladies of Gazebo admit *this* marquis limits himself to pinching the occasional bottom.

The second beautician takes control of the conversation again. "I think it's a unique experience that you can have only if you do adopt a ghost," she says firmly. "Little things happen, but it's nice. It's nice to have someone else around, and to know these things do exist."

Her colleagues nod, and the the final word on the subject is said: "It doesn't bother any of the clients. It's fun. If you work late at night by yourself

THAT'S INCREDIBLE!

you don't feel like you're alone."

Sande Marsolan loves to hear about the lives her clients and their newfound entities have made together. She's glad they've found the closeness she and her ghost, Jeffrey, have, and intends to keep up with her good work.

"I have adopted out more than one hundred ghosts," she says. "Some of them have been famous—like William Shakespeare, Veronica Lake, and the Marquis de Sade—but most are quite ordinary in their own extraordinary way.

"I would say that this agency is my life's work. I'm dedicated to this. I firmly believe in what I am doing and I truly, truly enjoy it. It has enriched my life tremendously.

"And I firmly believe in ghosts."

What do you think?

Are there really such things as ghosts? Is it possible to adopt one? And if it is possible—would *you* want to adopt a ghost?

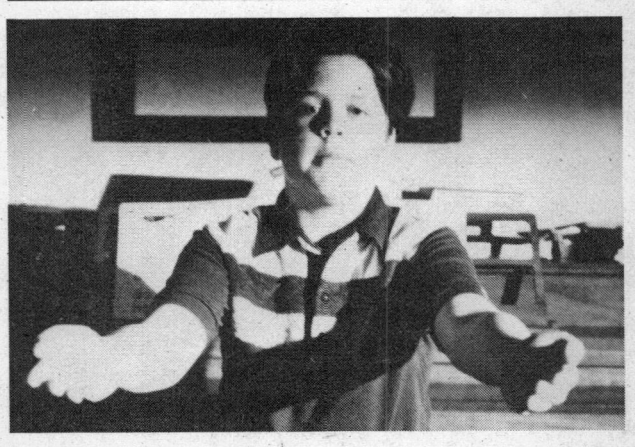

14. CLOSE ENCOUNTER

August 27, 1979. A car is driving west on County Road 5 near Highway 220 in Marshall County, Minnesota. The spot is some ten miles west of Stephen, Minnesota, and twenty-two miles northwest of Warren, where the nearest county sheriff's office is located.

It is a clear night, not starry but nevertheless not starless. The area beneath the blackened sky is rural, a stretch of land dotted with farms and farmhouses. The terrain is long and low, flat like Dutch countryside without the windmills. The highway takes the moving car through long, deserted miles, unmarked by buildings or even trees, no obstructions of any kind either north or south of County Road 5. Even the highway is deserted—except for its single, moving population of one. Other than the driver, there are no people visible; the early-to-bed-

THAT'S INCREDIBLE!

early-to-rise farmers are fast asleep and have been for hours. As the driver checks his watch, he sees the time is 1:40 A.M.

In the car is Val Johnson, at the age of thirty-five a happily married father of three—and for the past three years a deputy with the Marshall County Sheriff's Department. Pleasant-natured, mustachioed Val Johnson is not given to flights of fancy. Or fantasy.

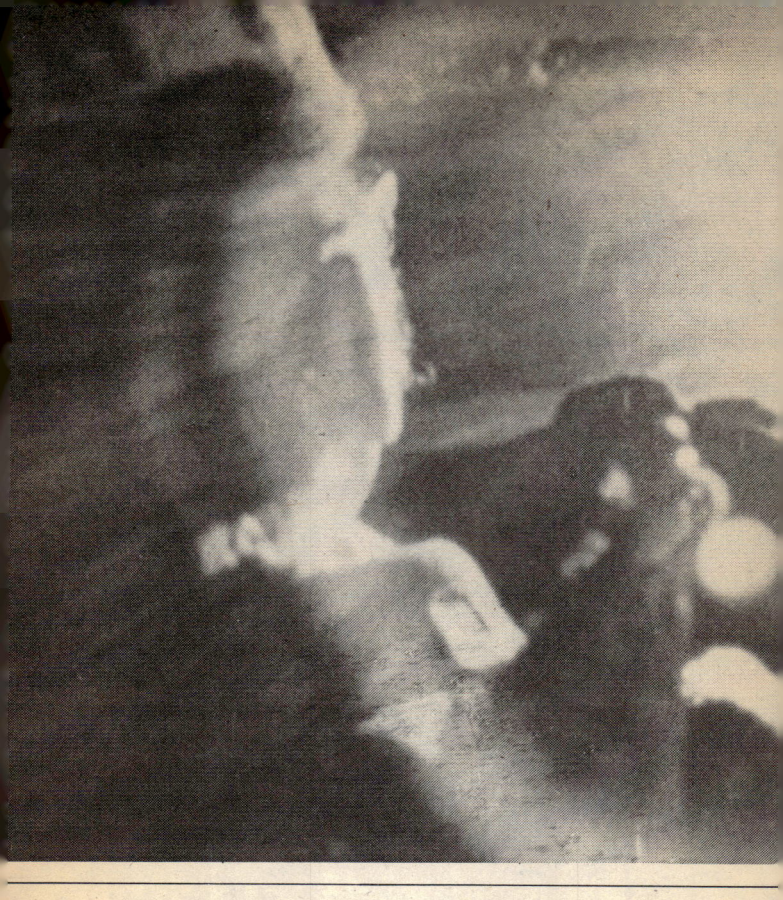

Still driving west, Val for the first time sights a bright light hovering about six feet above the ground. "A semi," thinks Val, "with a headlight out." Worth flagging down, ticketing, giving at least a warning?

As he drives on, Val changes his mind. It's not a semi at all, but there's a chance it's a downed airplane. And if that's so there may be survivors, and he presses his foot to the accelerator for the next

THAT'S INCREDIBLE!

half-mile.

The light appears at first to be motionless, but as he approaches Johnson notices that *it* has begun to speed up and is now racing toward *him*. There is no sound; only a blinding glare as the light hurtles toward him, and a last-minute sound of breaking glass before the last of the stars went out for Val Johnson. There his memories end.

••

169

When Johnson regained consciousness, he found his car had skidded sideways across the highway and stalled. He was hunched over, his forehead touching the steering wheel, and his eyes burned like wildfire in their sockets. He groped for the microphone that would put him in touch with the Sheriff's Department, and flipped the appropriate switch. As he did so, he thought at last to look for the hovering mass of light. Along with the memory of how he had lost consciousness, it was gone.

At the Sheriff's Department, radio dispatcher Deputy Peter Bauer flipped a switch that would allow him to respond to Val Johnson's call. The conversation was automatically recorded.

JOHNSON: 407.
BAUER: Go ahead, 407.
JOHNSON: 220-51.
BAUER: What is your condition?
JOHNSON: I don't know, something just hit my car. I don't know how to explain it. Strange.
BAUER: What's your condition? Are you okay?
JOHNSON: Something attacked my car. I heard glass breaking and the (unintelligible) locked. I don't know what happened.
BAUER: I'll get a hold of 406 and send him right away.

Number 406 was Deputy Greg Winskowski, who sped to the scence as soon as he learned of Johnson's predicament. He found Johnson still half-slumped over the steering wheel, and he pulled open the door.

"Val, what happened here?" he asked quietly, and helped Johnson into a sitting position.

THAT'S INCREDIBLE!

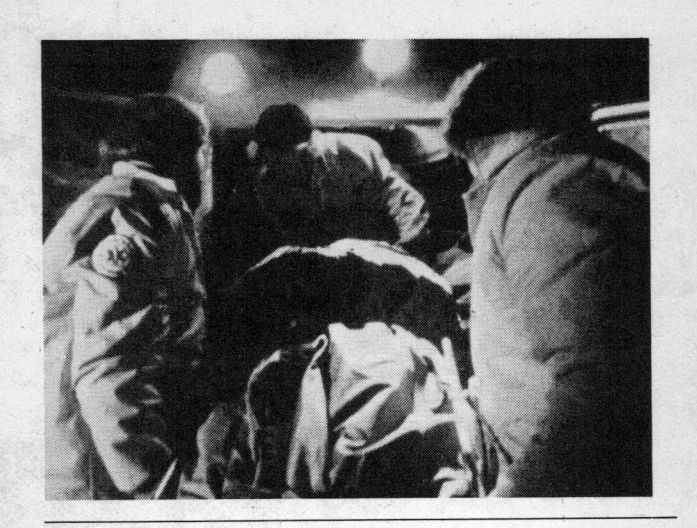

Johnson shook his head, still dazed, and said, "I don't know what the hell happened. Something attacked my car."

Winskowski noticed a red bump on Johnson's forehead. Seemed to him the man might be in a state of shock. "What kind of car was it?" he asked, as he helped Val out of the damaged car and into his own police car.

"It wasn't a car," Val replied, shaking his head again and trying to gain control of his legs. "I don't know what the hell it was."

Sheriff Dennis Brekke arrived at the scene after the two deputies had driven away, and drove Johnson's patrol car back to the department garage. Circling around it, whistling occasionally in total disbelief, he catalogued in his mind the damage he saw:

1. one headlight smashed to pieces;

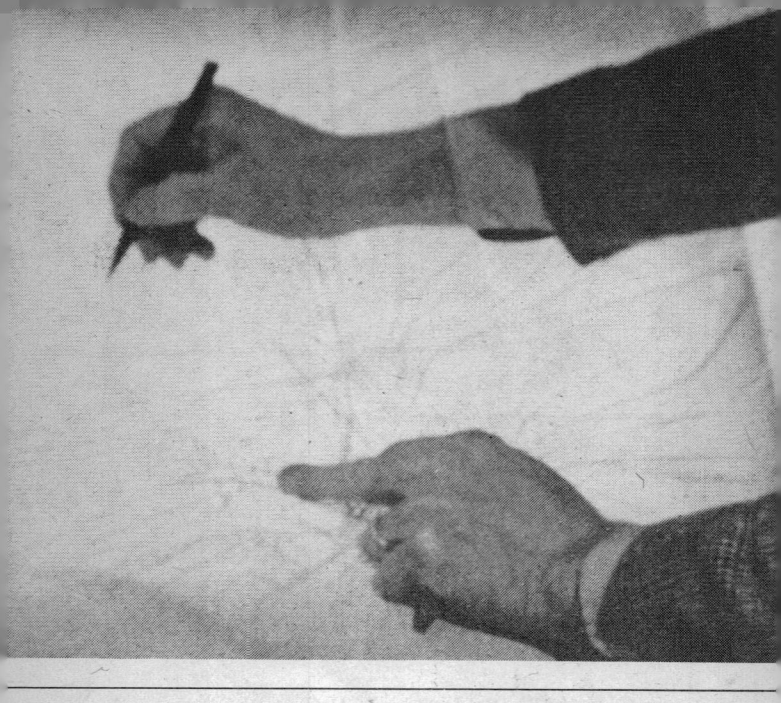

2. a small circular dent hammered into the upper hood;
3. the windshield shattered—yet still in one piece—in front of the steering wheel;
4. a whip antenna on the roof bent backward at its base;
5. a similar whip antenna on the trunk bent in its upper portion at a right angle; and
6. a red plastic light filter punctured and dislodged from its lamp housing.

What kind of wreck causes this kind of damage? thought the sheriff as he completed his mental inventory. No wreck I ever saw, was his final reply. Better get Val's story in the morning, he concluded, and locked the garage door behind him as he left

THAT'S INCREDIBLE!

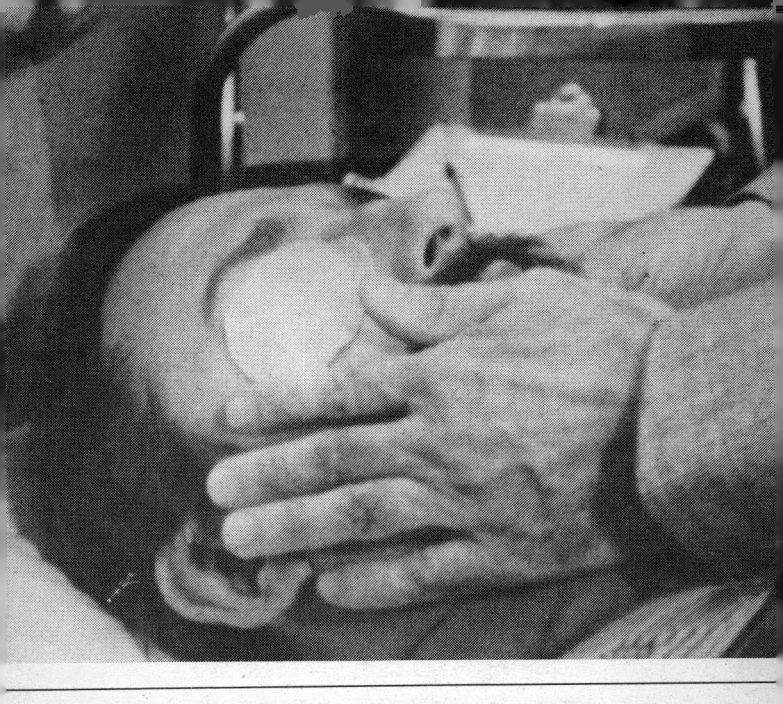

for home—after one last puzzled glance.

An ambulance had rushed Val to the hospital in Warren, and Dr. W.A. Pinsonneault checked him over for broken bones, concussion, the usual aftermath of a car wreck. But there were none.

"But my eyes are burning like crazy," Val had told the doctor, and thus Pinsonneault concentrated on the burning sensation. There seemed to be a pinkish irritation across the surface of both eyes; unable to do more, the doctor applied salve and bandages and sent Val Johnson home.

It was the end of the most extraordinary evening in the deputy's life.

What happened that night? What was it that hit Val Johnson's car? A UFO?

No one really knows. But the story doesn't end with just a string of question marks.

A call was placed to Allan Hendry, an investigator for the Center of Unidentified Flying Object (UFO) Studies. He came to Marshall County as soon as he heard the story of Val Johnson's incredible experience.

"We learned of the Val Johnson case in much the same manner we learn about most of our sighting reports," says Hendry. "The deputy of Marshall County contacted us directly via our 800 toll-free number, which we've issued to ten thousand police departments around the country."

But this one was more than usually interesting to Allan Hendry. "The case is very striking for the simple reason that a law-enforcement officer re-

THAT'S INCREDIBLE!

ported a sighting that left behind damage to his car and injury to his own eyes immediately following the accident." It is, of course, unusual for a policeman to be the one reporting he might have had contact with a UFO. Usually police are the first to calm fears of just such events by saying, "You must have been seeing things," or "Lamplights always look like UFOs on foggy nights."

"The biggest mystery about the Val Johnson case to me," continues Hendry, "is trying to find one neat explanation for something to behave the way he described it yet create the kinds of damage we've analyzed and discovered."

Hendry had asked the Ford Motor Company for assistance—Johnson's police car was a Ford—in detailing the nature of the damage to the car's windshield. The request filtered down through the company, and finally came to rest on the desk of

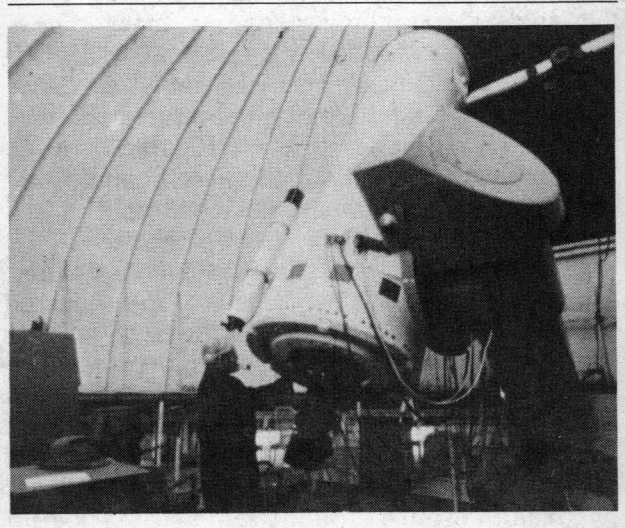

Meriden French, one of Ford's crash technicians.

"I was asked to come out and examine the windshield," he says. And that's just what he did. But the remarkable spiderweb of cracks and fractures baffled the glass expert as they had everyone else who had seen them. "The cracks in this particular windshield are not unusual in themselves. I could reproduce any one of them in the laboratory. But as a group..." He doesn't end the sentence.

But French did his best to identify the fractures, beginning by tracing the outline of the shattered windshield onto a piece of paper, the better to study the configurations. But even this led to no concrete conclusions. According to Meriden French: "I'm convinced that the fractures we see here were made by some sort of blow from the outside of the glass by some firm, probably hard, object, but not with sufficient force to bend the glass to the point of

THAT'S INCREDIBLE!

breaking it. I have not seen anything like this before. They're extremely unusual." His feeling was that the glass fractures were the result of mechanical forces rather than thermal stress.

And what of the strangely bent antennas?

At the material-testing lab of Minneapolis Honeywell in Minneapolis, Roland Wardell undertook the study of the two bent whip antennas. Using a stereo-optical microscope, he tried to determine if any deposits were left on the metal. Results seemed to be inconclusive, as no radioactive residue was found. But tests did not indicate a softening of the metal. It was finally concluded that the antennas might have been bent by a high-velocity air blast, and the hood indentations may have been caused by impact with airborne particles such as stones.

Possibly a large airborne object hovering above the ground, generating great heat and power and swirling around the stones and small objects beneath it? Something like an unidentified flying object?

Never for an instant did any of the supporting players in Val Johnson's drama doubt his story—that he truly had nothing to do with the damage to his car, and that he was completely unable to recall what had happened. The Sheriff's Department stood by him all the way.

"I've been in law enforcement for about fifteen years," said the chief deputy. "I've been chief deputy sheriff in Marshall County for eight years.

"I looked at that car myself. The car itself had busted headlights, the windshield was broken, one of the red lights was broken, the antennas were bent backward—whereas if an object had struck them they would have been bent forward, but they

THAT'S INCREDIBLE!

were bent the opposite way as if some force had bent them." He's perplexed, as is everyone else who sees what happened to Val's car. But as far as he's concerned, the damage has nothing to do with Val.

"Val Johnson is a very good fellow," he says. "He's a good officer, has three young children and a nice wife. He's a reliable person.

"My feeling is that whatever happened was strange and unknown. And there is no doubt in my mind that Val was telling what he actually saw."

But the jury remains out on the strange occurrence. And no matter how anyone tries, no one's yet offered a reason for what may be the strangest evidence of all: Val had set and synchronized his wristwatch and the clock in his car on the night the event took place. Both were correct when he left the garage that night. But later, after what happened on County Road 5, they were checked again. Both were exactly fourteen minutes slow.

Very possibly, what happened to Val Johnson that night was what astronomer J. Allen Hynek has labeled a "close encounter," a term coined nearly ten years ago to describe those UFO sightings that are relatively close by, usually within five hundred feet.

Such an experience can't possibly leave a man without impressions of his own, and Val Johnson speaks freely about what happened in the summer of 1979.

Upon reflection, he and his wife, Rozanne, have come to the conclusion that perhaps their Creator has created other creatures that we on Earth can't readily see or easily identify. Perhaps the thing he encountered on County Road 5 was one of these.

One would assume Johnson often encounters skeptics who don't believe his story. Oddly, he finds the opposite is the case, and he explains why.

"Since the story's become public there've been twelve or fifteen stories that have come to me from people in the same area where I work about similar occurrences that have happened over the last twenty years. People have come forward and said,

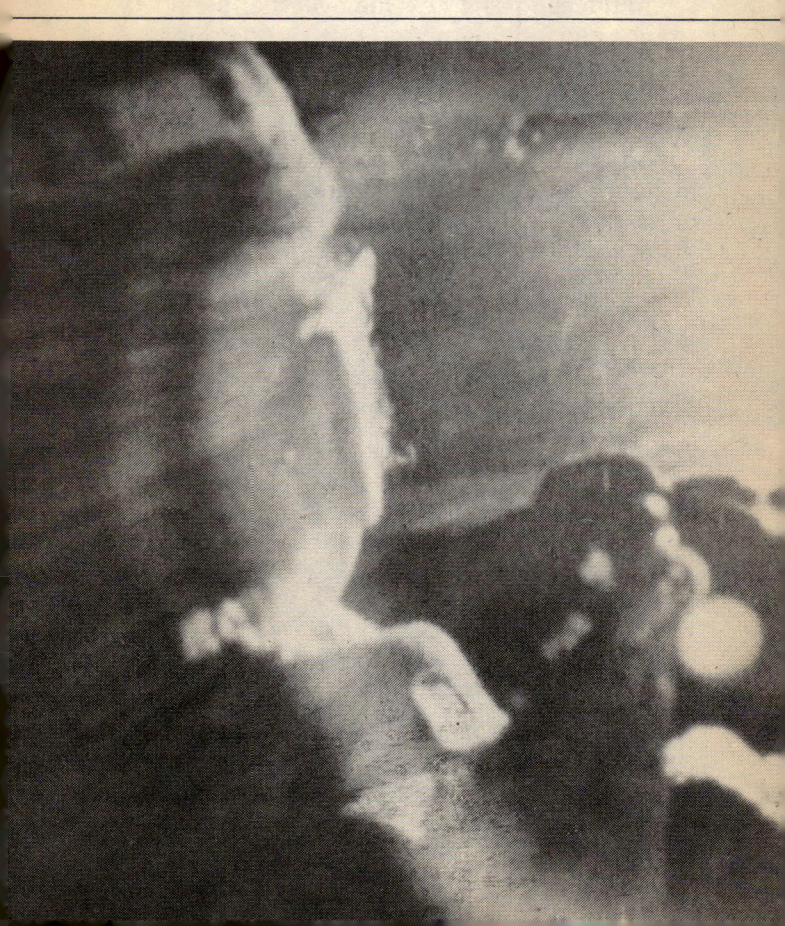

'Now that your story's public, I'll tell you what happened to me in '73 or '68 or even '28 . . .' Some strange things have been happening there."

So, decide for yourself. And if you're ever driving along County Road 5 in the vicinity of Highway 220 in Marshall County, Minnesota, drive carefully, and keep a good watch on the sky.

There's just no telling what you might see.

15. THE SMART PILL AND THE MOUSE

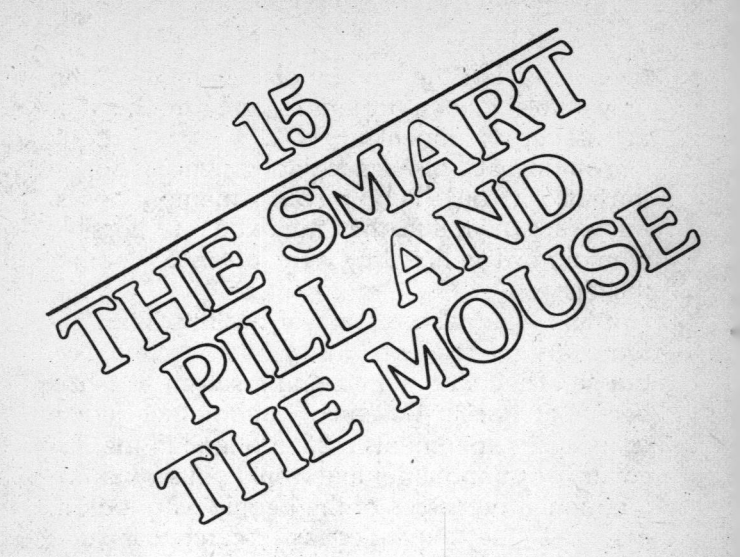

Do you get nervous just before finals, wondering how you're going to remember everything? Most students experience occasional binds where they have to absorb a lot of material for one reason or another, and they know it's not easy. Even older people sometimes get into memory problems: as the years go by they forget facts, faces, incidents, and generally can't put together all the pieces from their pasts. For the student or anyone else who draws a blank, memory lapses can be trouble—or at least very inconvenient.

You might be pleased to know science is hot on the trail of a way to help you out of memory lapses. Interestingly enough, they stumbled on a possible memory drug while they were looking for something else.

It all began with a team of health-science researchers at Creighton University in Omaha, Nebraska. They were continuing research that had begun at Pacific Research Laboratories fifteen years ago, experiments meant to lead to the discovery of a tranquilizer that would not slow down the mental processes of the people who took it. Eventually they expanded the research to include a search for chemicals that increase a person's brain-power. What Pacific Research came up with was a compound called PRL-8-53.

After preliminary studies showed that the compound *did* do good things for the brains of laboratory animals, and also showed that it was safe for use, the researchers at Creighton began to study it themselves. A preliminary study, led by Dr. Nikolaus Hansl, associate professor of medicinal chemistry in the Creighton School of Pharmacy, turned up some interesting results.

For a better look at Dr. Hansl's work, he invites you into his laboratory to meet—a mouse.

The mouse is nosing around in a small box separated into two parts. The box is an experiment in itself. Dr. Hansl is using the box and the mouse to prove that PRL-8-53 does something almost everyone could use: it improves the memory.

Mice are basically night-people—nocturnal

creatures—and they're more comfortable in the dark than in the light. Therefore, if given a choice between a bright area and a dark area, they'll instinctively move into the darker area. For that reason, there's a light in one side of the box, while the other side has no light fixture. A tiny door separates the two sides. The mouse begins in the brightly-lit area.

If the doctor opens the small door, the mouse will immediately go from the light side to the dark side. But once he gets there, there's a surprise in store for him. The doctor gives him a mild electrical shock. The shock is meant to tell the mouse that his instinct is wrong, that no matter what else he may think, the dark area *isn't* such a great place to be. After the shock has been administered, Dr. Hansl moves the mouse back to the lit side of the box and repeats the process.

The mouse is once again nosing around in the bright light, and Dr. Hansl opens the small door. Will the mouse remember the shock and stay where he is? Will he cross into the dark zone?

He's back in the dark zone in just six seconds. Dr. Hansl bypasses the electric shock, puts the mouse back in his cage, and turns his attention to a second mouse. Dr. Hansl puts this second mouse in the light side of the box. It's never been there before and it has no idea what to expect.

Now the doctor opens the door, and—no surprise here—the mouse goes directly to the dark side. The mouse gets the same shock the first mouse received, and then the doctor gently puts him back into the lit side of the box.

Dr. Hansl is about to repeat the experiment, but there's a slight twist: this mouse differs from the first in one very important way. A little earlier, this mouse was given a small dose of PRL-8-53. Will it remember the shock it received and steer clear of the unlit side of the box?

Let's see.

The doctor opens the door between the two compartments. The mouse approaches the door, but does not dash straight through as the first mouse did. As a matter of fact, this mouse resists its instincts for forty-eight seconds, nearly a full minute, before crossing into the dark side. Its memory of the shock is much better than that of the first mouse.

Experiments such as the ones involving mice are giving scientists much hope that they're onto something big, although there's still no sure proof that the compound will work on people.

But in 1979, at Creighton University, more than

PRL-8-53

a hundred students and faculty members allowed themselves to be used as human guinea pigs by taking part in a PRL-8-53 test. For the test, some students were actually given the compound while others were given placebos (which look like the real thing but have no effect of any kind). The students didn't know whether they had the real thing or just the placebo.

Said one subject, "After taking the pill I felt no change. I can't recall any change, or even whether I took the pill or not. I can't tell if I had the placebo."

Another subject's experience was very different. "After I took the pill I thought my memory had improved. I thought I was able to grasp things a little better."

A third subject explains the test he took. "The memory-pill test was a simple sequence of taped data, like number sequences," he says. "I remember listening to a tape of a sequence of numbers, and then I was supposed to repeat them. The sequence got a little longer, and then I was supposed to repeat *that* sequence of numbers."

This subject received a sequence of numbers, but other subjects at other times have also received lists of nonsense syllables they were expected to repeat, sets of geometric figures they were expected to reproduce, and similar tasks. The reason for using things like numbers, nonsense syllables, and geometric shapes is that everyone, all over the world, thinks of the same things when they hear numbers, for instance. The written numeral 3, for example, makes an American or a Chilean or an Eskimo think of exactly the same thing, as numbers are the same in all cultures. But the word "paella" makes a person of Hispanic extraction hungry, while it leaves a Dane cold—since he knows nothing of the delicious rice dish for which the word "paella" stands. The Spaniard will remember the word "paella" because it means something good in his culture. Since Dr. Hansl wanted to make sure all subjects would have an equal chance to remember the sequences, he used words—or non-words—that everyone would feel the same way about.

The investigators found that in all tasks, subjects did much better after taking PRL-8-53.

"If the statistics showed that I improved dramatically after taking the pill," said one blasé subject, "I'd be very much surprised."

And when he saw the results, which showed that he had improved by an incredible eighty percent after taking the drug, he was *plenty* surprised.

THAT'S INCREDIBLE!

"My goodness," he said, "that really is quite dramatic, really astounding. It's really exciting to see these results!"

When the experiment was over, Dr. Hansl heard one question over and over again: "When will this pill go on the market?"

Like most scientists, he's got an answer ready: "At the very earliest it will be two years," he says. "We'll just have to take it easy and be sure beyond a shadow of a doubt that, even with prolonged use, it will be as safe as we have reason to believe it is."

While he's making sure, thousands of forgetful people will be counting the days till Dr. Hansl's miracle memory drug comes to their drugstores. But in the meantime, help may be available in the form of a man with a truly incredible memory. His name is Harry Lorayne, and he's written an entire book on the subject of memory improvement.

Tell him you have a bad problem with names, that you forget them the minute you hear them, and he's ready to go.

"You just said the key word," he says. "We don't really forget names. You know what people do? They either don't remember them in the first place of else they never even *hear* them in the first place.

"Usually when you're introduced to someone, you hear a mumble, not a name. And you can't remember a mumble. People don't do the obvious, best thing, which is to say, 'I didn't hear your name.' They figure 'I'll never see this person again, so why bother?' But what often happens is that they *do* see that person again—the next day, week, month, year, or whatever—and that's why half the world calls the other half 'mac' or 'buddy' or 'sweetheart,' not because they're so endearing but because they don't know who the heck they're talking to."

After that rapid-fire answer he takes a quick breath and continues, "But that's all right, because the other half of the world doesn't know who's talking to them. Which means we *all* go through life with the blinkers on."

What Harry's trying to say is that we don't see with both eyes or listen with both ears, and there's probably a lot of truth in what he says.

Harry's perfectly willing to prove what the memory can do when it's helped out with a little concentration. One stunt he often pulls involves meeting for the first time a hundred or so people, and then an hour later—without cards or tricks or anything else, just sheer memory power—calling each and every one of those people by name. How does he do it? Well, the way Harry explains it, he just takes the trouble to hear the name, look at the face, and remember both.

Which, in this impersonal world, makes memory magician Harry Lorayne one very unforgettable guy.

THAT'S INCREDIBLE!